C000071606

For Better or For Worse
The Comic Art of Lynn Johnston

Lynn Johnston and Katherine Hadway
with an essay by Amber Landgraff

Goose Lane Editions and Art Gallery of Sudbury

Copyright © 2015 by the authors.
All rights reserved. No part of this work may be reproduced or used in any form or by any means, electronic or mechanical, including photocopying, recording or any retrieval system, without the prior written permission of the publisher or a licence from the Canadian Copyright Licensing Agency (Access Copyright). To contact Access Copyright, visit www.accesscopyright.ca or call 1-800-893-5777.

Edited by Paula Sarson.
Cover and page design by Julie Scriver.
Layout by Jaye Haworth.
Cover photo by Brian J. Tremblay.
Printed in Canada.
10 9 8 7 6 5 4 3 2 1

Goose Lane Editions acknowledges the generous support of the Canada Council for the Arts, the Government of Canada through the Canada Book Fund (CBF), and the Government of New Brunswick through the Department of Tourism, Heritage and Culture.

Goose Lane Editions
500 Beaverbrook Court, Suite 330
Fredericton, New Brunswick
CANADA E3B 5X4
www.gooselane.com

Library and Archives Canada Cataloguing in Publication

For better or for worse (Goose Lane Editions)
  For better or for worse : the comic art of Lynn Johnston / Lynn Johnston
and Katherine Hadway ; with an essay by Amber Landgraff.

Co-published by: Art Gallery of Sudbury.
ISBN 978-0-86492-864-1 (pbk.)

1. Johnston, Lynn, 1947- — Exhibitions.
2. Johnston, Lynn, 1947- For better or for worse—Exhibitions.
3. Cartoonists—Canada—Biography—Exhibitions.
4. Family—Comic books, strips, etc.—Exhibitions.
5. Parent and child—Caricatures and cartoons—Exhibitions.
6. Canadian wit and humor, Pictorial—Exhibitions.
7. Comic books, strips, etc.—Canada—Exhibitions.
I. Art Gallery of Sudbury, issuing body, organizer II. Title.
III. Title: Comic art of Lynn Johnston.

PN6733.J55Z75 2015   741.5'971   C2015-900798-4

Art Gallery of Sudbury
251 John Street
Sudbury, Ontario
CANADA P3E 1P9
www.artsudbury.org

To all young and aspiring cartoonists
from the teams at the
Art Gallery of Sudbury and *For Better or For Worse*

Cartooning is actually the oldest and most enduring art form,
going all the way back to the paintings in the Chauvet-Pont-d'Arc Cave in France
and the hieroglyphs of ancient Egypt. They tell the story of everyday life in their time,
just as cartoonists do today, and will continue to do in some form
until there are no humans left to chronicle . . . and lampoon.

— Wiley Miller
Non Sequitur

Contents

11 **Foreword**
by Karen Tait-Peacock

13 **Once Upon a Pencil**
by Lynn Johnston

15 **The Comic Art of Lynn Johnston**
by Katherine Hadway

169 **Growing Up with the Pattersons**
An Evolution of Style in *For Better or For Worse*
by Amber Landgraff

183 **Acknowledgements**

185 **Bibliography**

187 **Illustration Credits**

189 **Index**

Foreword

The Art Gallery of Sudbury is very proud to present this retrospective publication and exhibition of North Bay–based artist Lynn Johnston as part of our efforts to present, interpret, and celebrate the work of Northern Ontario artists.

Johnston is most well known for her enormously popular comic strip *For Better or For Worse* that appeared from 1979 to 2010 in the first instance in newspapers, and then in anthologies and collections, and eventually as animated cartoons. That the strip is now rerun from its beginning attests to its enduring appeal to a new generation of parents, grandparents, and children trying to cope with change and the chaos of family life.

The exhibition offers a close look at the life and career of this remarkable Canadian artist, in particular the sources and development of *For Better or For Worse*. Our purpose is to show that this comic strip was not created from scratch. On the contrary, it grew from many influences: from Johnston's family, from her own life, from the example of many popular cartoonists who produced work daily and weekly for publication in newspapers and for the colour comics of the Sunday papers, and also from resources as diverse as *MAD* magazine.

I would like to express my sincere thanks to all the people who have taken part in organizing this publication and exhibition, which helps to chart a new path in understanding Johnston and the creative contexts in which she worked and from which her art continues to grow. Our deepest debt is to Lynn Johnston, her daughter Kate, their families, and staff who so enthusiastically embraced our vision and worked so hard to help us realize it.

The Art Gallery of Sudbury wishes to gratefully acknowledge those who have contributed toward this publication and the exhibition, including the *For Better or For Worse* Team: Lynn Johnston, Katherine Hadway, Stephanie van Doleweerd, Greg Wotton, Kevin Strang, and Ghislaine Dean; the Goose Lane Editions team: Susanne Alexander, Julie Scriver, Martin Ainsley, and Paula Sarson; and guest curator Deanna Nebenionquit.

The Gallery wishes to acknowledge the generous support of Canadian Heritage, FedNor/Industry Canada, Ministry of Northern Development and Mines, City of Greater Sudbury, Greater Sudbury Development Corporation, Vale, Canada Council for the Arts, and the Ontario Arts Council.

To the Art Gallery of Sudbury staff, Board of Directors, past Chair Alan Nursall, and to countless volunteers and supporters who have helped in immeasurable ways, thank you.

by KAREN TAIT-PEACOCK, Director
Art Gallery of Sudbury

Once Upon a Pencil

by LYNN JOHNSTON

I don't think anyone begins a career as a cartoonist. As one possible option drifts into another, you simply fall into it. A cartoonist is "that way" from birth. A cartoonist is in training for a lifetime: watching cartoons on TV, appreciating the antics of expressive, storytelling relatives, and trying anything to get laughs. A cartoonist is an entertainer. More often than not, a cartoonist's childhood behaviour is considered annoying and irritating, but it is here — amidst family, teachers, and friends — that funny stuff is tested, reworked, polished, and honed. Being called "class clown" is a compliment. A teacher can't demean a budding cartoonist with admonishments such as, "You'll never make a living by telling jokes, my friend! . . . Do you think you're funny?" The answer to this is, "Yes, I think I could make a living telling jokes . . . because I *am* funny!" It's in the blood. It's in the mind and in the heart, and it's unmanageable for the longest time. Then, you find your medium and you hit your stride. Where this skill takes you is often a surprise.

For thirty years, I had the privilege of writing and drawing a syndicated comic strip. I met my heroes, and I used every gift I was given. I worked harder than I thought was possible, and I had the time of my life. *For Better or For Worse* was another existence, another personality — the other side of me. I thought it would be difficult to say goodbye to an alter ego, but when it was time for the story to end, I ended it. Without looking back, I let my comic strip family go. For a while.

13

A year ago, I received an invitation from the executive director and chair of the Art Gallery of Sudbury in Ontario. I was asked if I would consider doing a touring show of my cartoons. Wow. Having been told by two other curators that my work was not "art," such a thought had not occurred to me. I was surprised, curious, and then, motivated! Not only were they interested in displaying my syndicated work, but also they asked if they could include drawings from my childhood, my days as a commercial artist, and even the work I'm doing now. That's a lot of material!

With the goal of a touring show in mind, my daughter and two friends have taken on the formidable job of filtering through more than fifty years of drawings, doodles, sketches, and scrawl. They are finally making headway. The boxes have labels now, and the work has been carefully archived and stored. I must admit, I am overwhelmed by the care being taken of work I had just set aside and ignored.

I have so many people to thank for breathing life back into a career I thought had ended with the final panels of a comic strip. I am redrawing things that were damaged, creating new illustrations, and bringing my fictional family (in a small way) to life again. I am also playing with new ideas, and I think I am ready to let you see what they are.

I thought I had retired. I thought I might paint realistically, begin a new identity as a "fine artist," but it hasn't been happening. I can't rid myself of the stuff I was born with: the need to be silly and to work for a laugh. I am still a cartoonist, and even if some folks don't call it fine art, it's fine with me. I have had the best life ever!

The Comic Art of Lynn Johnston

by KATHERINE HADWAY

For nearly thirty years, the Patterson family has lived and grown with us, as though they were just another ordinary family. The difference is: they exist only on paper. The fictional family at the heart of Lynn Johnston's comic strip *For Better or For Worse* has seen its share of ups and downs, highs and lows. Unlike other comic strips, Lynn's characters grew and changed in real time. Perhaps this is one of the reasons why *For Better or For Worse* has been so successful, and why it has resonated with so many people, and for so long.

The story has revolved around Elly Patterson, a married housewife and mother of three. What began as a family-based, gag-a-day type comic strip evolved into a sophisticated, storyline-based, dramatic column that addressed everything from chores and relationships to death and spirituality. It has been discussed over morning coffee in millions of households across Canada, the United States, and beyond for over three decades and is still gaining new readership since 2008, when the strip began to run again from the beginning in newspapers and online. *For Better or For Worse* has become part of people's daily lives and routines, taking on a life of its own and cementing its popularity.

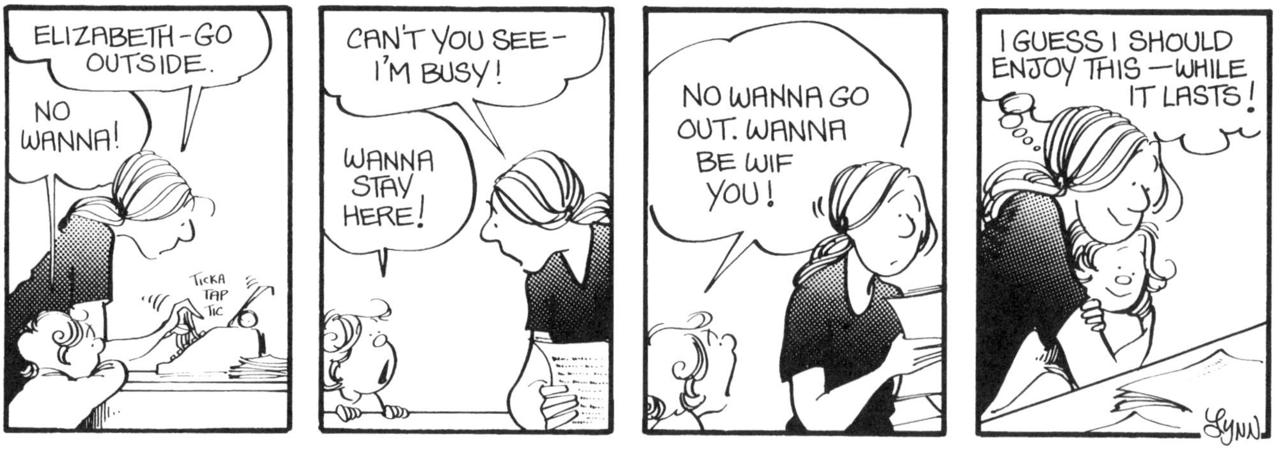
ELIZABETH-GO OUTSIDE.
NO WANNA!
TICKA TAP TIC
CAN'T YOU SEE- I'M BUSY!
WANNA STAY HERE!
NO WANNA GO OUT. WANNA BE WIF YOU!
I GUESS I SHOULD ENJOY THIS —WHILE IT LASTS!
LYNN

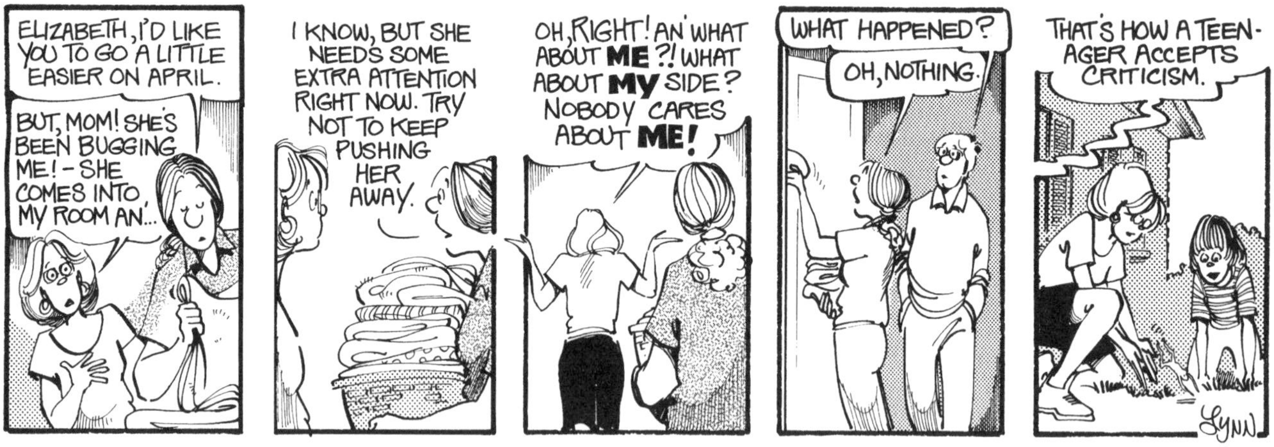
ELIZABETH, I'D LIKE YOU TO GO A LITTLE EASIER ON APRIL.
BUT, MOM! SHE'S BEEN BUGGING ME! -SHE COMES INTO MY ROOM AN'...
I KNOW, BUT SHE NEEDS SOME EXTRA ATTENTION RIGHT NOW. TRY NOT TO KEEP PUSHING HER AWAY.
OH, RIGHT! AN' WHAT ABOUT ME?! WHAT ABOUT MY SIDE? NOBODY CARES ABOUT ME!
WHAT HAPPENED?
OH, NOTHING.
THAT'S HOW A TEEN-AGER ACCEPTS CRITICISM.
LYNN

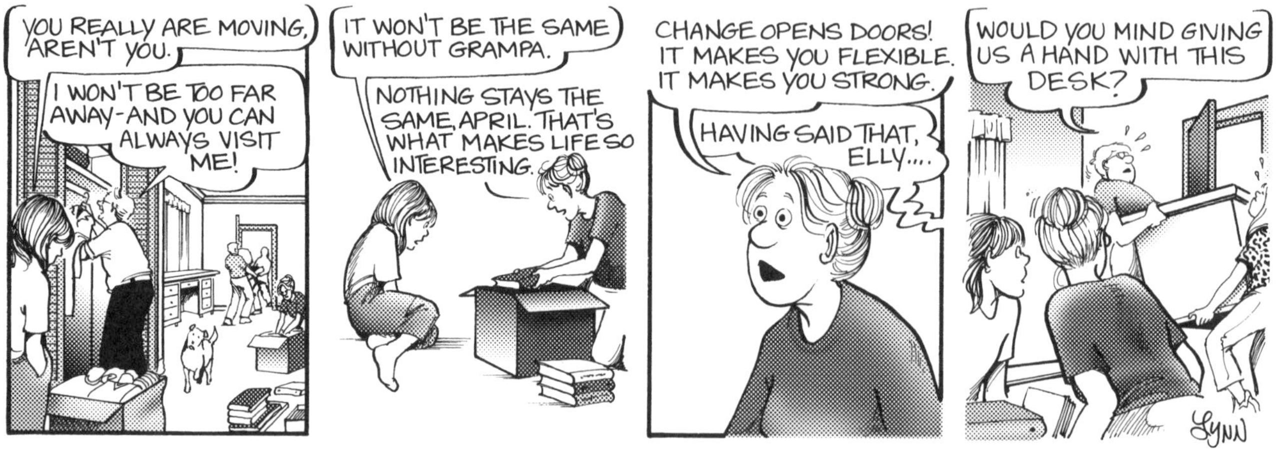
YOU REALLY ARE MOVING, AREN'T YOU.
I WON'T BE TOO FAR AWAY-AND YOU CAN ALWAYS VISIT ME!
IT WON'T BE THE SAME WITHOUT GRAMPA.
NOTHING STAYS THE SAME, APRIL. THAT'S WHAT MAKES LIFE SO INTERESTING.
CHANGE OPENS DOORS! IT MAKES YOU FLEXIBLE. IT MAKES YOU STRONG.
HAVING SAID THAT, ELLY....
WOULD YOU MIND GIVING US A HAND WITH THIS DESK?
LYNN

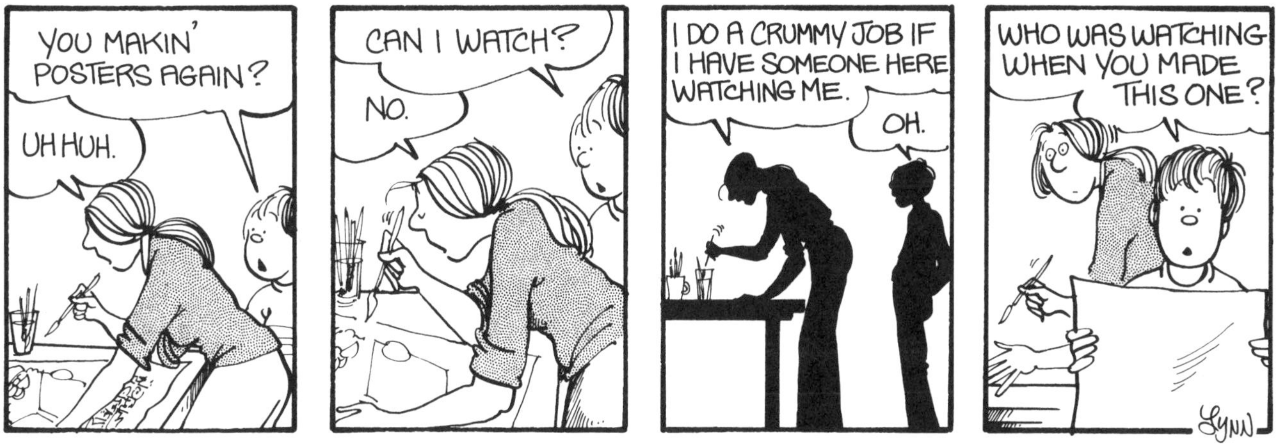
YOU MAKIN' POSTERS AGAIN?
UH HUH.
CAN I WATCH?
NO.
I DO A CRUMMY JOB IF I HAVE SOMEONE HERE WATCHING ME.
OH.
WHO WAS WATCHING WHEN YOU MADE THIS ONE?
LYNN

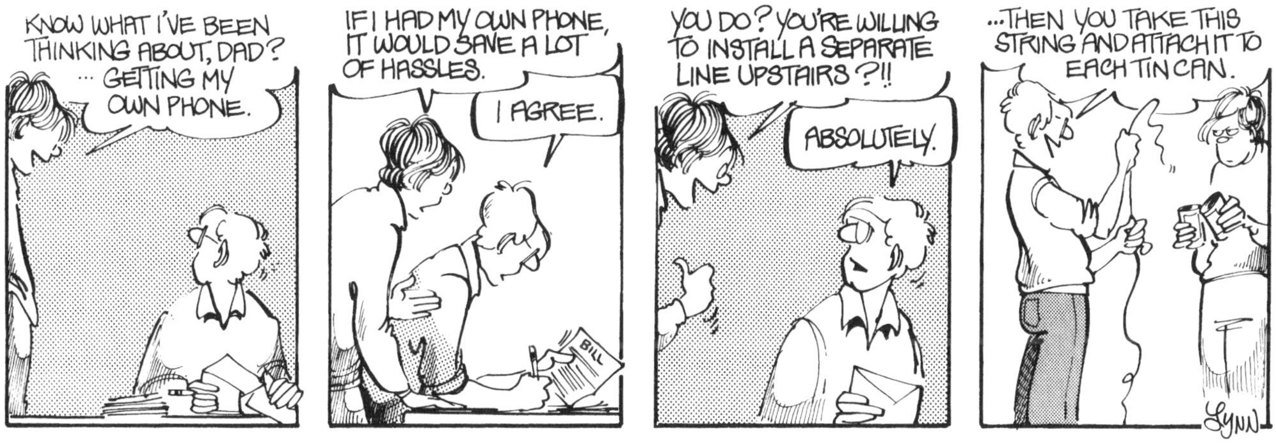
KNOW WHAT I'VE BEEN THINKING ABOUT, DAD? ... GETTING MY OWN PHONE.
IF I HAD MY OWN PHONE, IT WOULD SAVE A LOT OF HASSLES.
I AGREE.
BILL
YOU DO? YOU'RE WILLING TO INSTALL A SEPARATE LINE UPSTAIRS?!!
ABSOLUTELY.
...THEN YOU TAKE THIS STRING AND ATTACH IT TO EACH TIN CAN.
LYNN

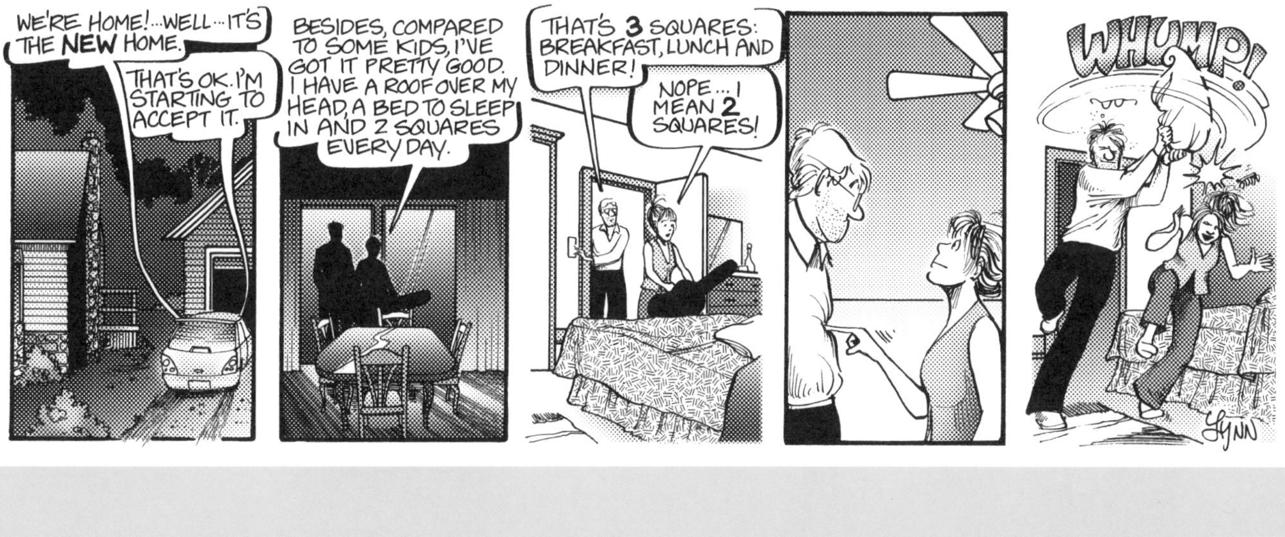
WE'RE HOME!...WELL...IT'S THE NEW HOME.
THAT'S OK. I'M STARTING TO ACCEPT IT.
BESIDES, COMPARED TO SOME KIDS, I'VE GOT IT PRETTY GOOD. I HAVE A ROOF OVER MY HEAD, A BED TO SLEEP IN AND 2 SQUARES EVERY DAY.
THAT'S 3 SQUARES: BREAKFAST, LUNCH AND DINNER!
NOPE... I MEAN 2 SQUARES!
WHUMP!
LYNN

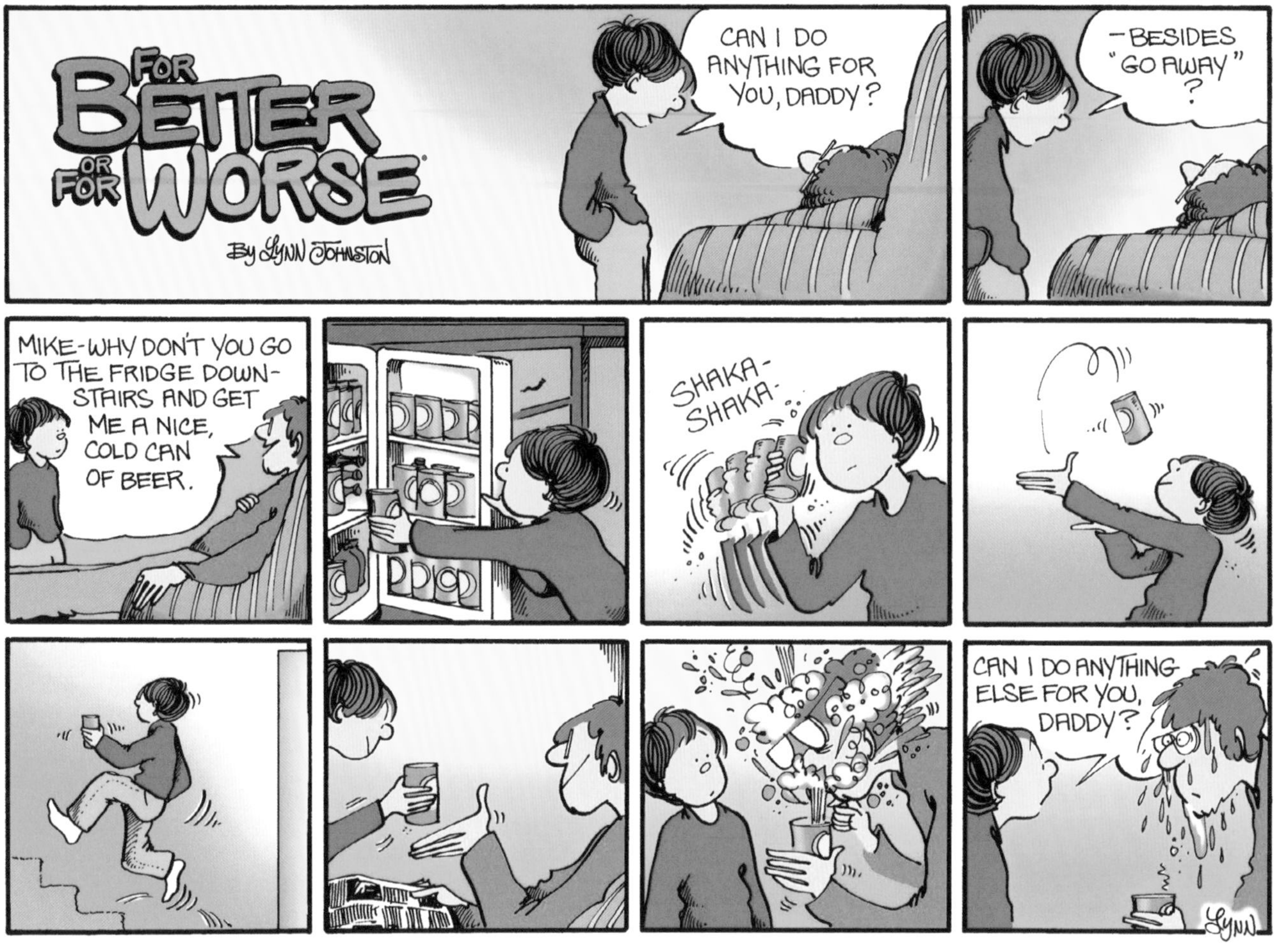

FOR BETTER OR FOR WORSE
BY LYNN JOHNSTON
CAN I DO ANYTHING FOR YOU, DADDY?
–BESIDES "GO AWAY"?
MIKE–WHY DON'T YOU GO TO THE FRIDGE DOWN-STAIRS AND GET ME A NICE, COLD CAN OF BEER.
SHAKA-SHAKA-
CAN I DO ANYTHING ELSE FOR YOU, DADDY?
LYNN

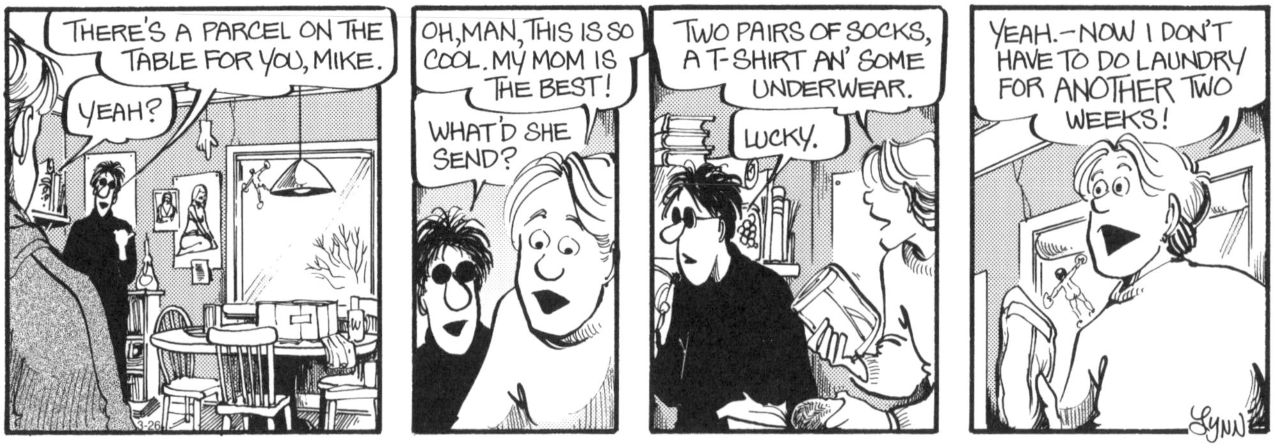

THERE'S A PARCEL ON THE TABLE FOR YOU, MIKE.
YEAH?
3-26
OH, MAN, THIS IS SO COOL. MY MOM IS THE BEST!
WHAT'D SHE SEND?
TWO PAIRS OF SOCKS, A T-SHIRT AN' SOME UNDERWEAR.
LUCKY.
YEAH.–NOW I DON'T HAVE TO DO LAUNDRY FOR ANOTHER TWO WEEKS!
LYNN

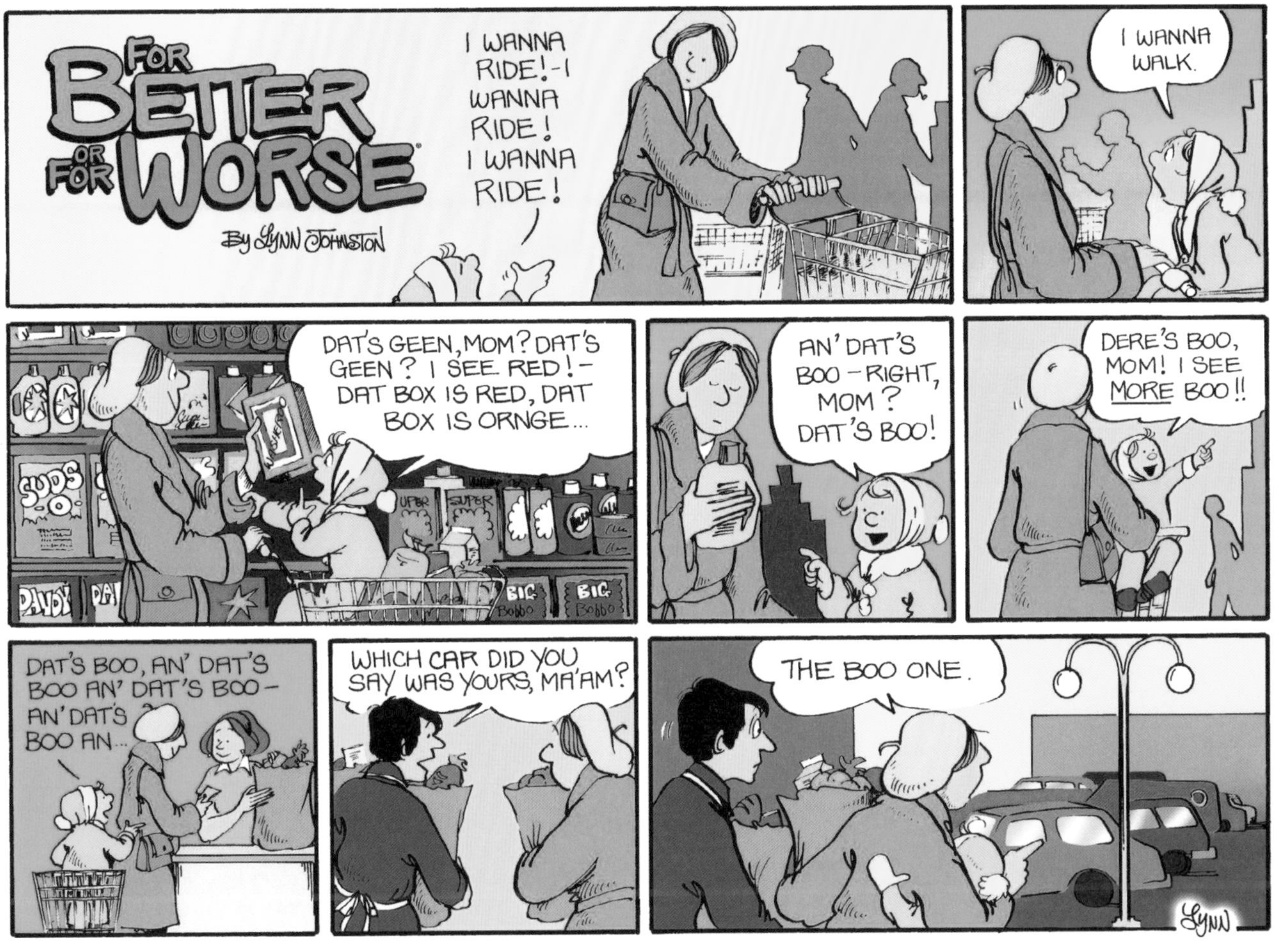
FOR BETTER OR FOR WORSE
BY LYNN JOHNSTON
I WANNA RIDE! - I WANNA RIDE! I WANNA RIDE!
I WANNA WALK.
DAT'S GEEN, MOM? DAT'S GEEN? I SEE RED! - DAT BOX IS RED, DAT BOX IS ORNGE...
AN' DAT'S BOO - RIGHT, MOM? DAT'S BOO!
DERE'S BOO, MOM! I SEE MORE BOO!!
DAT'S BOO, AN' DAT'S BOO AN' DAT'S BOO - AN' DAT'S BOO AN...
WHICH CAR DID YOU SAY WAS YOURS, MA'AM?
THE BOO ONE.
LYNN

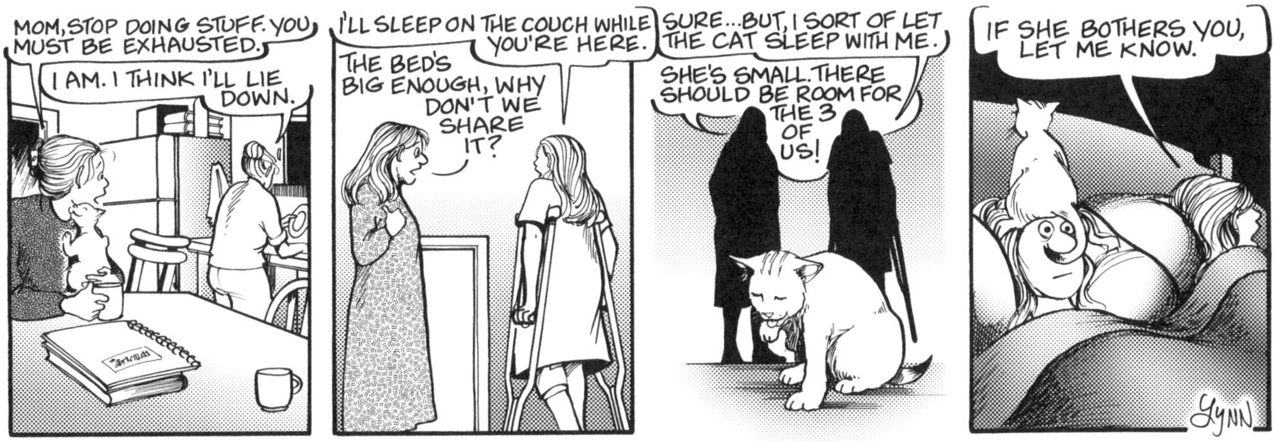
MOM, STOP DOING STUFF. YOU MUST BE EXHAUSTED.
I AM. I THINK I'LL LIE DOWN.
I'LL SLEEP ON THE COUCH WHILE YOU'RE HERE.
THE BED'S BIG ENOUGH, WHY DON'T WE SHARE IT?
SURE...BUT, I SORT OF LET THE CAT SLEEP WITH ME.
SHE'S SMALL. THERE SHOULD BE ROOM FOR THE 3 OF US!
IF SHE BOTHERS YOU, LET ME KNOW.
LYNN

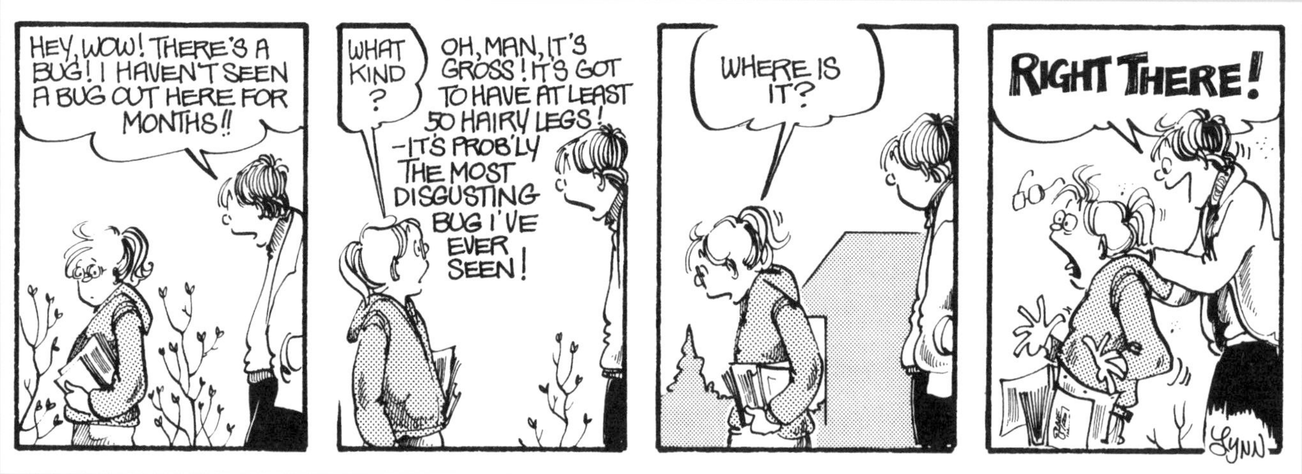
HEY, WOW! THERE'S A BUG! I HAVEN'T SEEN A BUG OUT HERE FOR MONTHS!!
WHAT KIND ?
OH, MAN, IT'S GROSS! IT'S GOT TO HAVE AT LEAST 50 HAIRY LEGS! –IT'S PROB'LY THE MOST DISGUSTING BUG I'VE EVER SEEN!
WHERE IS IT?
RIGHT THERE!
LYNN

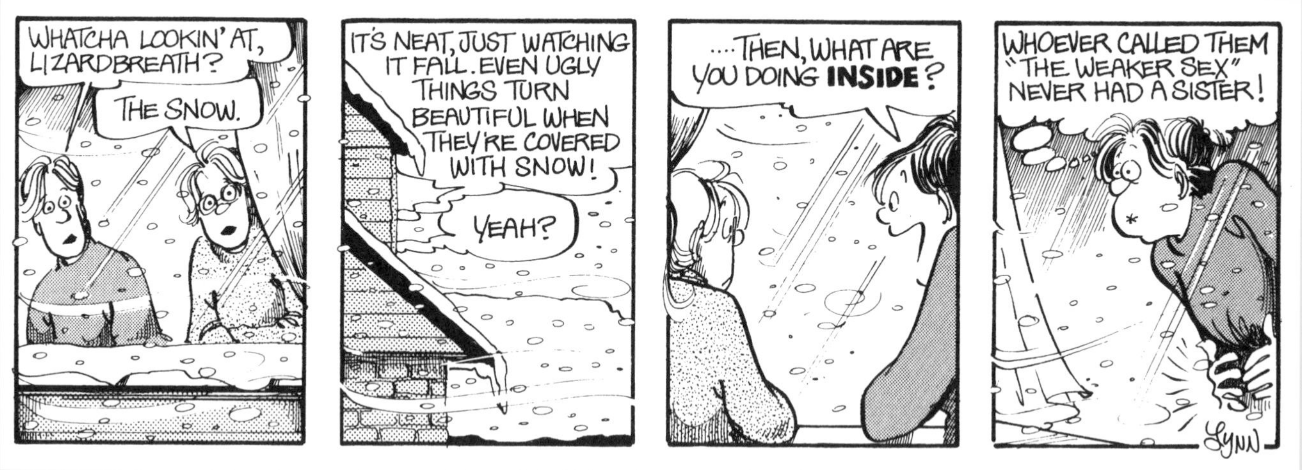
WHATCHA LOOKIN' AT, LIZARDBREATH?
THE SNOW.
IT'S NEAT, JUST WATCHING IT FALL. EVEN UGLY THINGS TURN BEAUTIFUL WHEN THEY'RE COVERED WITH SNOW!
YEAH?
....THEN, WHAT ARE YOU DOING **INSIDE**?
WHOEVER CALLED THEM "THE WEAKER SEX" NEVER HAD A SISTER!
LYNN

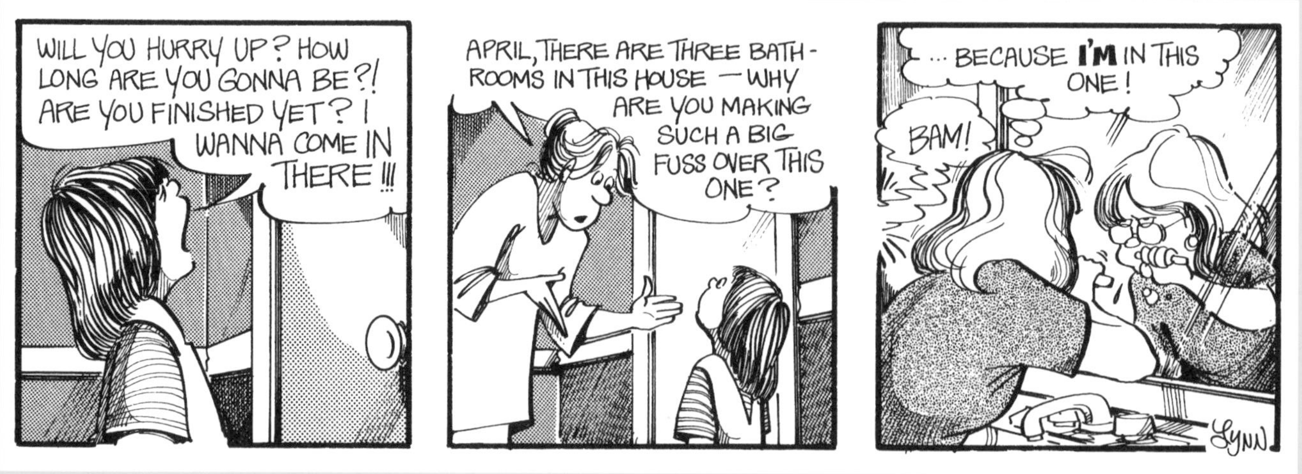
WILL YOU HURRY UP? HOW LONG ARE YOU GONNA BE?! ARE YOU FINISHED YET? I WANNA COME IN THERE!!!
APRIL, THERE ARE THREE BATHROOMS IN THIS HOUSE — WHY ARE YOU MAKING SUCH A BIG FUSS OVER THIS ONE?
... BECAUSE **I'M** IN THIS ONE!
BAM!
LYNN

"FINDING" SUCCESS

There is no question that Lynn and *For Better or For Worse* have been successful, but when she is asked how it happened, her response seems too simple: "When a door was opened, I seized the opportunity." She says her good fortune evolved because people opened doors for her. But it wasn't as simple as that. Her success has been the result of hard work, high standards, passion, and determination. Lynn has been interviewed countless times, and how her comic career began and developed is well documented. What is not clear is who exactly the key players (or characters) have been in this success story? Who has graciously opened doors for Lynn, and who has slammed them shut? What has she taken away from these situations, good and bad, and how have they helped to shape not only Lynn's life and career but also the characters and the storylines in *For Better or For Worse*?

HOW DID IT ALL BEGIN?

Lynn was born in 1947 in Collingwood, Ontario, a railway and port town located on the shores of Georgian Bay, roughly two hours north of Toronto. Her parents, Mervyn and Ursula Ridgway, had met in England during the Second World War; they were both enlisted in the Royal Canadian Air Force and met in England on an air force base. After the war, they were married and settled down in Collingwood, where her father had been raised. Lynn still has a number of relatives living there.

Mervyn and Ursula Ridgway, 1946.   Lynn, age three, and Alan, age one.

Homesick for her family on the West Coast and unable to feel at home in the small town her husband loved, Ursula insisted the family move west. Lynn, age two, and her newborn brother, Alan, were uprooted and moved to North Vancouver. Unsettled and without the opportunities he enjoyed in Collingwood, Lynn's father found work in the City of Vancouver as a watchmaker and a jeweller. Ursula busied herself with the children, managed the household, and occasionally worked for her father in his stamp business.

Ursula Ridgway was a talented artist. She could draw, paint, sew, sculpt, and create almost anything. She was also a highly skilled calligrapher.

> [She] had been trained as Granddad's private secretary before she left home during the war, and did the painstaking illustrations and calligraphy that made some of his customers' stamp collections among the most beautiful and valuable in the country.
>
> I watched for hours as she inscribed with India ink on the fine cream-coloured paper. [...] I learned to love the characters she drew even before I recognized them as the alphabet.

Lynn's father loved comic art. He had a collection of cartoon books, and even though the cost of taking the family to a movie was prohibitive, he would splurge when a good comedy came to town. He enjoyed music, too. He spent much of his spare time with his children, singing wartime songs, playing the guitar, and reading aloud. He delighted in puns, limericks, slapstick gags, and comedic performance. With an entertainer on one side and a conservative on the other, the Ridgways were a rather mismatched couple.

I inherited my mother's ability to draw, and from my father, I inherited the love of silliness. Music and a good laugh are the things he live[d] for. He was born to entertain, to story tell. I don't believe he's forgotten a joke he's ever heard. In fact, despite my mother's rather Victorian upbringing, she too had a gift for puns and wordplay. If my parents did not communicate with the openness and directness one expects today, they communicated with humour. If you can't say it right out . . . joke about it.

(right) Pencil sketch by Ursula (Bainbridge) Ridgway, along the Fraser River, 1938.

(below) The characters Grandpa Jim and Grandma Marian were modelled after Lynn's parents.

Perhaps it was the lack of family communication, or maybe it was Lynn's unwillingness to do what she was told — either way, young Lynn found herself occupying much of her time in her room. This is where she discovered her joy of drawing.

In my room, which I shared with my younger brother, were toys and books and junk, but my real escape was paper. I hoarded it. I kept old greeting cards, box tops, notepaper — anything I could draw on, and in a state of wakeful dreaming, I would see images appear, my imagination come to life, my right hand drawing my thoughts on paper.

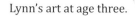

Lynn's art at age three.

While Lynn put her creative energy into drawing, her brother, Alan, focused his time on music. He became a professional trumpet player, composer, and teacher. Now that he is retired, he makes beautifully handcrafted wooden canoes and kayaks. Alan's music, wit, and personality later emerged as the character Uncle Phil, who was one of the more popular characters in *For Better or For Worse*.

The Ridgway Family, West Vancouver, 1955.

There were other talented family members who influenced young Lynn as well. Her mother, Ursula, was the middle of three sisters. The youngest, Monica Reznick, lived in Montreal with her husband and four children. She, too, was a capable artist. Lynn loved her for her candid conversation. In a family that buried serious feelings, where "we don't talk about those things, dear," was the answer to many questions, Monica's openness was exceptional. Lynn looked forward to the rare occasions when Monica and her family would come to the West Coast to visit.

Some of Lynn's earliest memories are of her mother's eldest sister, Unity Bainbridge. Unity was one of the early graduates of the Vancouver School of Art, where Lynn eventually began her training. By the mid-1950s, Unity was an established (albeit unorthodox) artist with a unique style that Lynn appreciated and admired.

> I was an artist. There was no question about it. I was going to be an
> artist like my Aunt Unity. Everyone said so and I knew it was true.
> I had been able to draw since the age of two. I accepted it.

Unity travelled all over British Columbia, capturing the integral character of First Nations people, their villages, their churches, and their surrounding landscape. Lynn remembers all corners and spaces of her aunt's small house filled with her art.

Little Indian Patient, Unity Bainbridge, pastel, 1943, 42 x 33 cm.

> Paints, drawing tools, and other supplies covered the
> dining-room table. Paintings, sketches, finished and
> unfinished work were stacked against the walls in every
> room. I was fascinated as much by Unity's painting
> and drawing equipment, as I was by the art itself.
>   Unity travelled with a flat wooden box, which
> folded out onto a small set of legs. Inside this box were
> her paints, brushes, and all the things she needed to
> sketch with. This box sat like a briefcase in her painting
> studio, a small, bright room on the side of her house.
> I knew that someday, I would have all of these things to
> work with too.

Lynn eventually took particular notice that Unity carried out her own marketing. In the 1960s she had begun to create prints, illustrated books about her travels, and greeting cards, all of which were popular items in galleries and specialty shops where tourists went to find exclusive examples of Canadian West Coast art. She was an irresistible force, promoting her work at a time when being an artist was discouraged by those who believed it was no way to make a living. Lynn saw in her "Aunt Unie" an example of a full-time working artist, who was able to blend her passion for beauty and expression with her ability to produce a line of work others could readily enjoy. Bainbridge, now ninety-eight years old, states, "I loved painting, capturing the truth in nature and in people. I was immensely grateful to be recognized with the Order of British Columbia in 1993." Unity Bainbridge had set the bar for Lynn.

Despite her family's abundant artistic talent and humour, Lynn recalls being a relatively negative child with low self-esteem. She partly attributes this to her mother's inability to show approval and appreciation towards her children. Lynn determined that Ursula's family did not believe in compliments. On the contrary, they believed praise discouraged people from striving to do better.

My mother never praised us — at least not to us personally. She might brag to a friend, but to us she would say it wasn't good enough. "That's a nice story you wrote, but the ending isn't good enough." "That's a nice pie you baked dear, but the crust is too soggy." And so on. I grew up thinking that nothing I did was good enough and that I wasn't good enough either. It took me a lifetime to get over this insecurity and to eventually believe that I was capable of doing something worthwhile.

Lynn's openness, over the years, about her tenuous relationship with her mother has, at times, caused friction within the family. The people who were close to Ursula adored her. Her downfall, in Lynn's eyes, was that she really didn't know how to deal with children. Unfortunately, by the time Lynn had reached an age Ursula could handle, the damage had already been done, and Lynn had broken away from her mother. The issues within their relationship would never truly be resolved. The silver lining from this relationship is Lynn developed an insatiable hunger to strive to do better: to draw better, to write better, to be funnier.

SHE'S THE TEACHER'S PROBLEM NOW!

By the time she reached school age, it was evident that art was a key element in Lynn's life. Not only had it given her an outlet, but it had also given her a level of confidence (and cockiness), which landed her in the principal's office far too many times.

> I loved to draw funny pictures. If they got me into trouble, it was worth it. If they made people laugh, I was high. By the time I was in my teens, I knew I would be a cartoonist. I never imagined, however, that I would someday have the great fortune (and awesome responsibility) of producing a comic feature that would be read daily by millions of people worldwide.

Teachers especially were a constant target for Lynn, a never-ending source of material.

Newspaper editorial cartoons during the 1950s and '60s were a prominent form of commentary, and her father had introduced her to the art of caricature. She drew caricatures of her father, of herself (using a mirror), and of her mother, who took it in good stride. It was inevitable that her teachers would be next. One teacher's likeness was attached to a dartboard, which was then delivered to the school principal. The unavoidable lectures preceding the detentions often went like this: "You can draw so well, Lynn, why don't you do something nice for a change," and, "Do you *want* to get yourself in trouble?" She admits that she did.

A caricature of Lynn's high school gym teacher, Miss Tate, whom Lynn and her friends preferred to call "Mistake."

(left) Lynn at roughly age ten, sporting a Toni perm, which she recalls didn't grow out for months.

(right) When Lynn was twenty-one, she aspired to write a book for kids about herself growing up. She was going to call it, "When I Was Lindy." Lindy was her childhood nickname, until she begged everyone to call her "Lynn." This is how she saw her ten-year-old self.

Lynn acknowledges she was a capable student, but it was a challenge for teachers to engage her in the subject being taught. She would doodle and daydream and make comments to disrupt the class. Lynn was no stranger to strict, swift discipline. When her grade 1 teacher, Mrs. Hindmarch, gave her "the strap," she knew it was time to toe the line. Lynn would push her teachers to their breaking points to see what she could get away with and discover where their boundaries lay. She admits the teachers she worked hardest for were the ones who stood their ground. She was testing everyone around her: teachers, family, and friends. Mrs. Hindmarch was the first person of authority outside the family to channel Lynn's energy away from misbehaviour and encourage her ability to draw.

Many years later, when her comic strip was well known, Lynn was able to make contact with the Hindmarch family by putting their name in the strip. When Mrs. Hindmarch called to say, "I'm sure you don't remember me," Lynn replied, "Not only do I remember how you looked and what you wore, you drove a pale blue, two-door Studebaker with the licence plate CBJ 386!" For thirty years that plate number appeared on the fictional "Pattersons'" car in *For Better or For Worse*!

(above and facing page) A few examples of where Lynn used Mrs. Hindmarch's licence plate number, CBJ 386.

Lynn describes herself by grade 4 as a superhero. When a weaker kid was bullied, Lynn came to the rescue with punches and with puns. Her mother's sharp tongue, and her use of the wooden spoon as a disciplinary tool, had taught Lynn to settle disputes with her fists. Word games had given her cutting wit and a fast comeback. Early on in George Stibbs's grade 4 class, however, she knew she had met her match.

An illustration from Lynn's book concept "When I Was Lindy." Based on a real scenario, Lynn depicted herself holding down a neighbourhood boy, who had been regularly teasing Alan, who stuffs grass into the boy's mouth.

Mr. Stibbs was a short man with a wry smile and a sweet disposition — I knew he'd be a pushover. The day I entered his class, I thought I had him pegged. His opening remarks to the class went something like, "I'm a tolerant guy, girls and boys. I don't mind a bit of conversation. I don't mind you moving about. As long as you pay attention and do your work, I'm a flexible man. The one thing I will not tolerate under any circumstances, however, is chewing gum. Anyone caught chewing gum in my class will be in a lot of trouble. So, if that's clear, let's get down to work."

Naturally I came to school the next day with a wad of gum in my mouth, ready to test his rule. As I chewed, he quietly approached my desk, kindly put a handkerchief under my chin and said, "Out." The class carried on. I figured I was home free, but after school as I was leaving, he stopped me and said, "Lynn, I have a few papers to work on after school today. I've called your mom and she says it's fine if you keep me company. And, while you are at your desk, I'd like you to write a few lines — you know, 'I will not chew gum in class,' . . . five hundred times should do it."

This was fine with me. I had good cursive handwriting, and loved to see the words flow vertically down the foolscap, " I I I will will will not not not," and so I began.

"Oh, and while you're at it," he said, "I brought you a present." He set on my desk an entire box of Fleer bubble gum. "I'd like you to chew these," he smiled, "every one of them."

The chewing was fun for a while. I chewed and wrote, "I will not chew gum… I will not chew gum." If he saw me faltering, he'd gently offer a handkerchief for the gum in my mouth, then he'd unwrap another cube and tell me to open up. When the box was half gone, I said I couldn't chew another piece. The taste was making me gag. But he kept opening the wrappers and gently popping the gum in my mouth. This was all done with kindness, good humour, and affection. By the time I had finished the entire box, I knew I would never chew gum in his class again, and I would also work harder for him than I had for anyone else! The best marks I ever got were in fourth grade — and to this day, I can't stand the smell of that gum!

George Stibbs taught Lynn to listen and to respect. It also was Mr. Stibbs who introduced her to limericks. Lynn found any poem that told a story, with a beginning, a middle, and an end, was entertaining and easy to remember. She discovered well-written lyrics were also poetry. Mr. Stibbs had his class listen to the music from *Carousel*, *Annie Get Your Gun*, and *My Fair Lady* just to experience the poetry.

Having been raised on *Winnie-the-Pooh*, *The Cat in the Hat*, and *Rupert*, I was already in love with rhyme. My dad's repertoire of British poems such as *The Lion and Albert* and songs like "Have Some Madeira, M'Dear,"

A clever turn of phrase would often get Lynn (and later, her offspring) in or out of trouble.

made me laugh till I cried. "The Cremation of Sam McGee" was equally entertaining, and having heard it so often, I found it easy to memorize.

I confess that poetry became less interesting to me after I left grade school. It wasn't until I discovered Shel Silverstein's work, first in *Playboy* and then in books like *Where the Sidewalk Ends*, that once again poetry made me laugh till I cried. Where there is good poetry, there is good writing; where there is good writing, there's an audience. I learned to write comic dialogue through an appreciation for good, rhyming poetry.

As a small token of thanks for having made such an impression on her, Lynn later wrote Mr. Stibbs into the strip — something she liked to do from time to time.

Lynn acknowledges she has many teachers to thank for giving her boundaries, guidance, and encouragement, and she remembers them all. One of the teachers she remembers fondly was her drama teacher, Thérèse Theriault.

Miss Theriault was one of Lynn's most memorable teachers.
("Norseman," North Vancouver Senior Secondary School Annual, 1964)

Lynn at age sixteen.

When I was in grade 8 I took my troubles to a young teacher who listened without lecturing, who gave me the courage to believe in myself at a time when I felt lost and confused about everything.

Lynn remembers grade 8 as a watershed year. Art and drama classes were well established at Sutherland Junior High in North Vancouver. Art, drama, music, and creative writing were as important as sports and academics, and Lynn found herself at home with like-minded people — both students and staff.

Thérèse was from Montreal, which immediately made her interesting. She was beautiful and funny and French. She made Shakespeare come alive; she also made poetry meaningful and rich with sentiment. She gave us freedom to write our own dramas, to star in and direct our own shows. She identified our strengths and gave us the courage to stand out when, as teenagers, we were pressured to be average and to fit in. Going from elementary school to the next level up was both terrifying and wonderful.

Those of us with a silly streak and a penchant for trouble needed all the help we could get. Thérèse was the right person in my life, at the right time. Instead of reining in our boisterous need for attention, she gave us the tools with which we could take our out-of-control energy and make it work *for* us for a change! She gave us permission to seek the spotlight and the ability to know what to do with it.

Besides Lynn, two other students in her eighth-grade drama class were destined for a career in comedy: Michael VadeBoncoeur and Paul Willis became Lynn's close friends and accomplices.

Michael lived a few blocks away from the school. At lunch hour we would take off and listen to records in his living room. There was a stack of 78s next to his dad's old record player, and every one was a comedy show. We listened to Harry Secombe, *The Goon Show*, Spike Jones, Tom Lehrer, and Stan Freberg. We made up our own songs and parodies. We wrote plays and what we called "black-outs" . . . kind of fast, three-statement gags, which ended with us exiting behind a black curtain. Most of our acts were terrible, but we had a wonderful time, and our teacher, Thérèse, kept telling us we had talent!

Lynn, Michael, and Paul entered high school together, but the atmosphere at North Vancouver Senior Secondary School was different. The arts were not a priority. Deprived of the art and drama classes they loved, the three comedians became a problem for the dedicated yet conservative Mrs. Watson, who was in charge of the high school art program.

We tormented her. She was a wonderful character, with the kinds of facial expressions and body gestures that were perfect for imitation. With a shake of his head, a slight wave of his hand, and an English accent, Michael could turn into a perfect Mrs. Watson. Aware of the pantomime and the popularity of our spoofs, she grit her teeth and gave us an education in spite of ourselves. She had us try sculpture and printmaking. We used oil paint and dyes. Within the limited budget of the school art department, she taught us about pottery and plaster, woodcarving and watercolour. She gave us an appreciation for different styles of painting, introduced us to the masters, and gave us wonderful lectures on the history of art.

But we were bent on her destruction, and more than once we brought her to tears. I feel badly about it now, but that's what we did.

Michael and Paul,
circa 1970.

With Michael and Paul as the writers and Lynn as the illustrator, the trio began a graphic novel about a love affair between Mrs. Watson and a math teacher down the hall. They called their book "The Blushbottom Memoirs." In retrospect, Lynn admits it was both juvenile and inappropriate. It kept them interested in Mrs. Watson's class, but Michael was expelled from the school well before their tome was complete. He had written a love letter to another boy, which at the time was a very serious offence. Michael disappeared without warning — he was transferred to another school. Paul transferred schools around that time as well, but Lynn never knew why. The three jokers were not to meet again until they were adults living in Ontario.

Lynn's caricature of Mrs. Watson is also the cover image
of the unpublished "Blushbottom Memoirs."

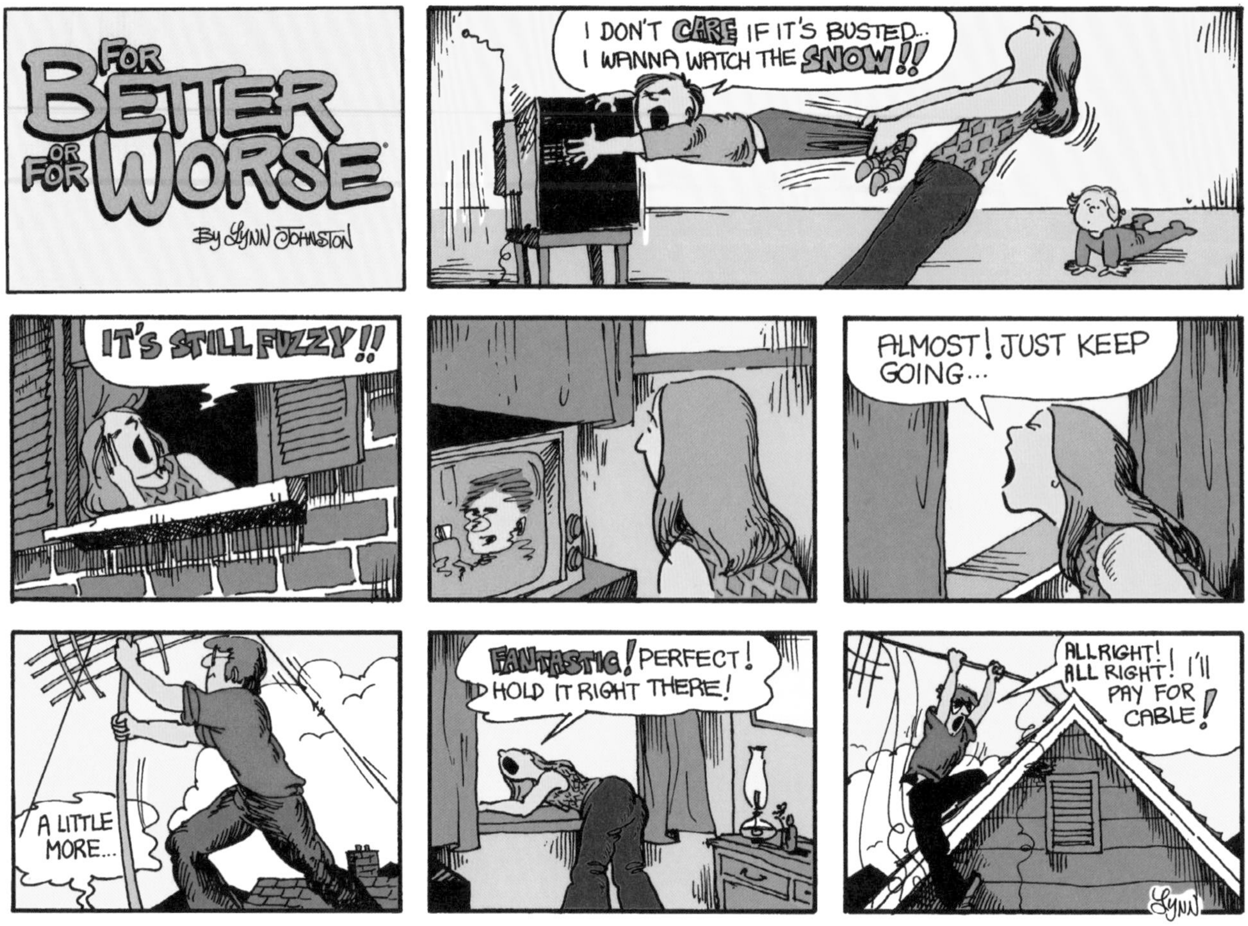
FOR BETTER OR FOR WORSE
BY LYNN JOHNSTON
I DON'T CARE IF IT'S BUSTED.. I WANNA WATCH THE SNOW!!
IT'S STILL FUZZY!!
ALMOST! JUST KEEP GOING...
A LITTLE MORE...
FANTASTIC! PERFECT! HOLD IT RIGHT THERE!
ALLRIGHT! ALL RIGHT! I'LL PAY FOR CABLE!
LYNN

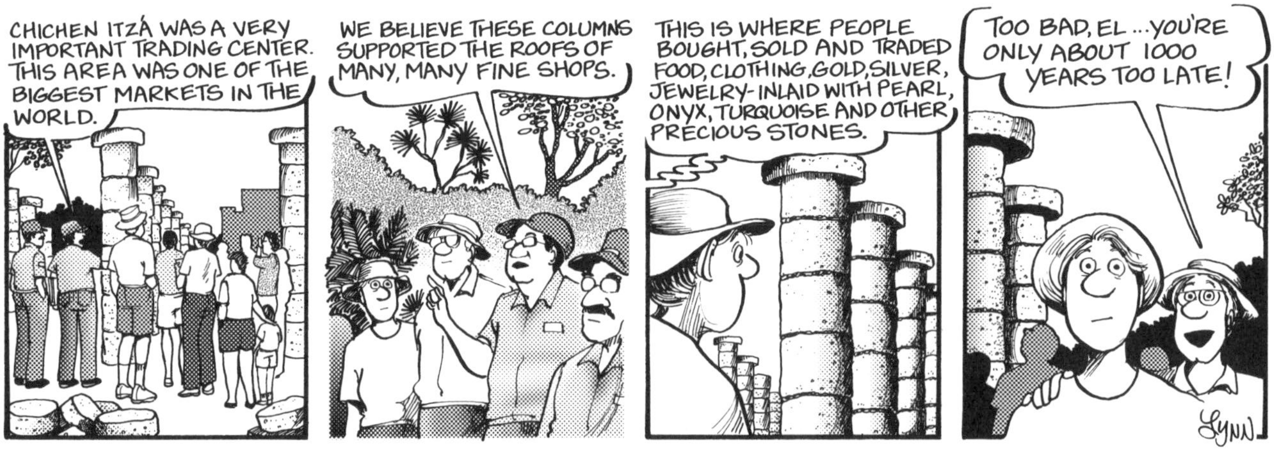
CHICHEN ITZÁ WAS A VERY IMPORTANT TRADING CENTER. THIS AREA WAS ONE OF THE BIGGEST MARKETS IN THE WORLD.
WE BELIEVE THESE COLUMNS SUPPORTED THE ROOFS OF MANY, MANY FINE SHOPS.
THIS IS WHERE PEOPLE BOUGHT, SOLD AND TRADED FOOD, CLOTHING, GOLD, SILVER, JEWELRY- INLAID WITH PEARL, ONYX, TURQUOISE AND OTHER PRECIOUS STONES.
TOO BAD, EL...YOU'RE ONLY ABOUT 1000 YEARS TOO LATE!
LYNN

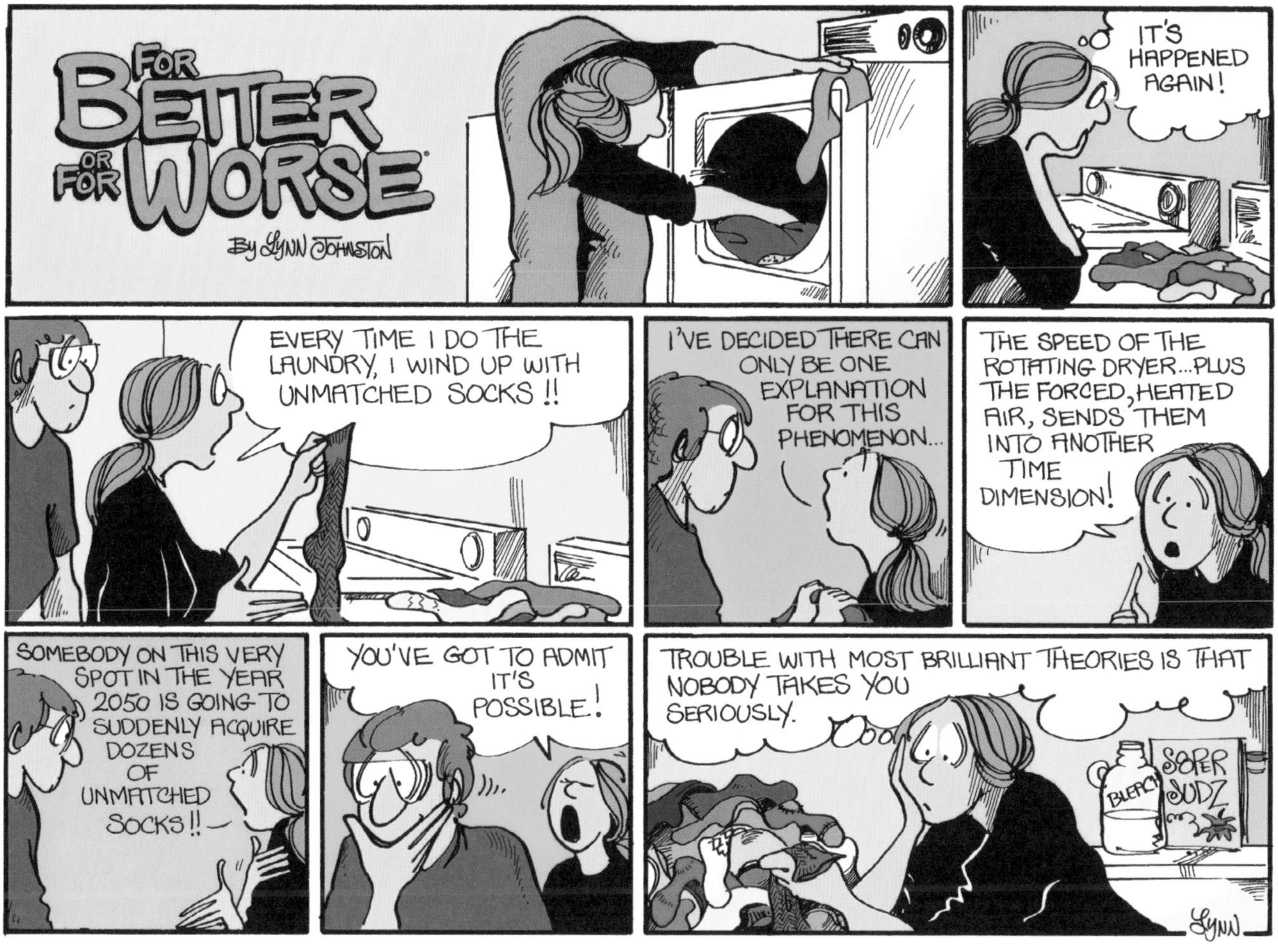
FOR BETTER OR FOR WORSE
By Lynn Johnston
IT'S HAPPENED AGAIN!
EVERY TIME I DO THE LAUNDRY, I WIND UP WITH UNMATCHED SOCKS !!
I'VE DECIDED THERE CAN ONLY BE ONE EXPLANATION FOR THIS PHENOMENON...
THE SPEED OF THE ROTATING DRYER...PLUS THE FORCED, HEATED AIR, SENDS THEM INTO ANOTHER TIME DIMENSION!
SOMEBODY ON THIS VERY SPOT IN THE YEAR 2050 IS GOING TO SUDDENLY ACQUIRE DOZENS OF UNMATCHED SOCKS !!
YOU'VE GOT TO ADMIT IT'S POSSIBLE!
TROUBLE WITH MOST BRILLIANT THEORIES IS THAT NOBODY TAKES YOU SERIOUSLY.
BLEACH
SOPER SUDZ
Lynn

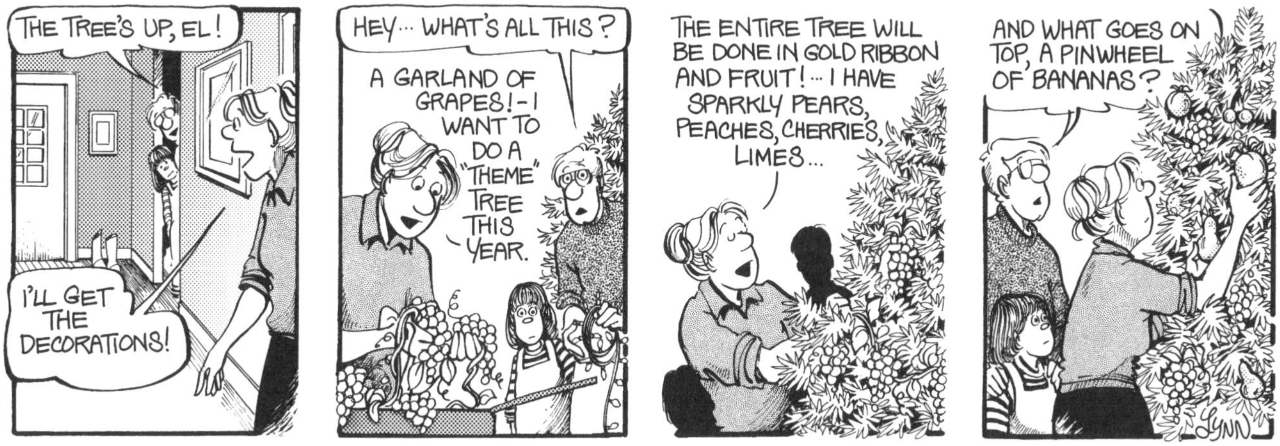
THE TREE'S UP, EL!
I'LL GET THE DECORATIONS!
HEY... WHAT'S ALL THIS?
A GARLAND OF GRAPES! - I WANT TO DO A "THEME" TREE THIS YEAR.
THE ENTIRE TREE WILL BE DONE IN GOLD RIBBON AND FRUIT! ... I HAVE SPARKLY PEARS, PEACHES, CHERRIES, LIMES...
AND WHAT GOES ON TOP, A PINWHEEL OF BANANAS?
LYNN

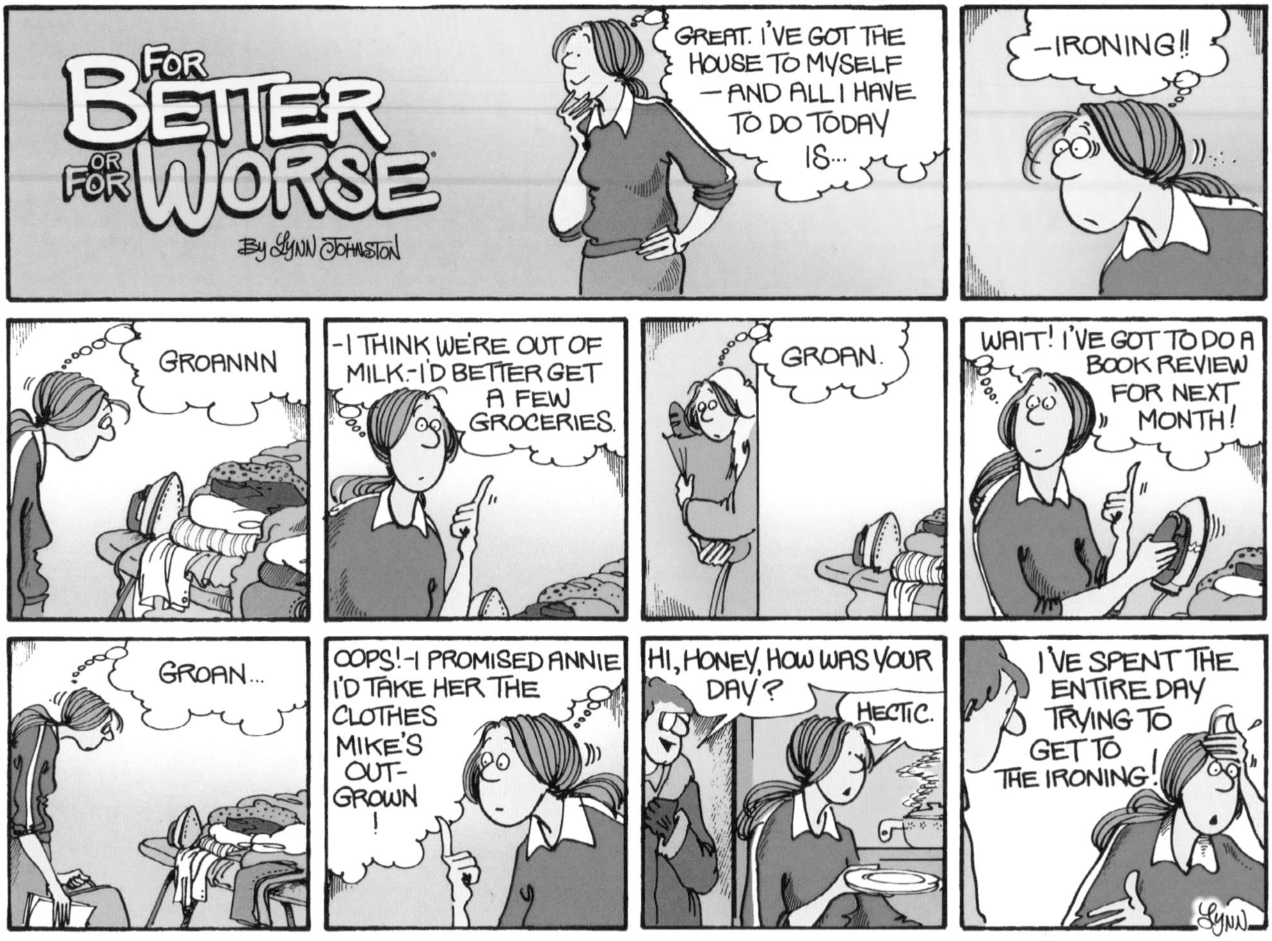
FOR BETTER OR FOR WORSE
BY LYNN JOHNSTON
GREAT. I'VE GOT THE HOUSE TO MYSELF —AND ALL I HAVE TO DO TODAY IS...
—IRONING!!
GROANNN
-I THINK WE'RE OUT OF MILK.-I'D BETTER GET A FEW GROCERIES.
GROAN.
WAIT! I'VE GOT TO DO A BOOK REVIEW FOR NEXT MONTH!
GROAN...
OOPS!-I PROMISED ANNIE I'D TAKE HER THE CLOTHES MIKE'S OUT-GROWN!
HI, HONEY, HOW WAS YOUR DAY?
HECTIC.
I'VE SPENT THE ENTIRE DAY TRYING TO GET TO THE IRONING!
LYNN

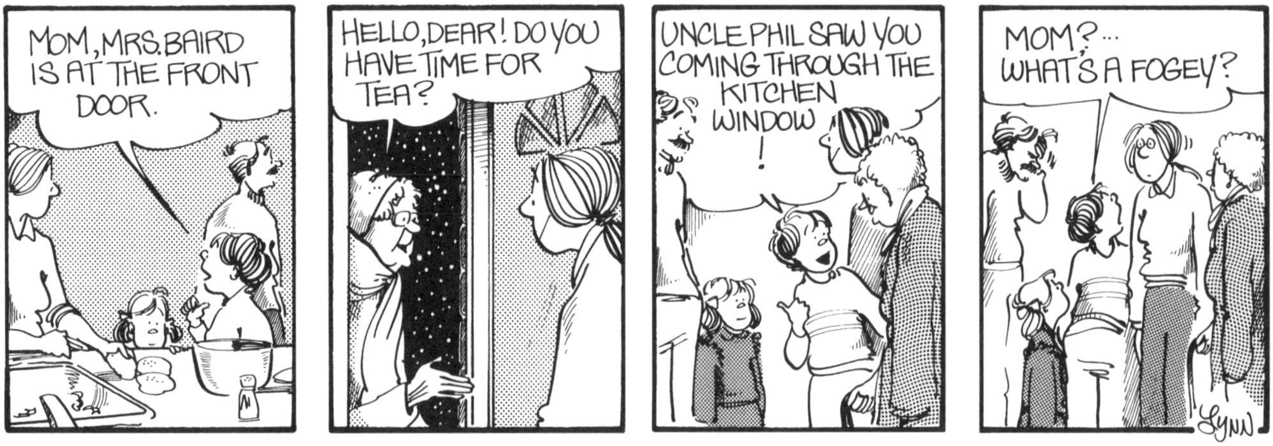
MOM, MRS.BAIRD IS AT THE FRONT DOOR.
HELLO, DEAR! DO YOU HAVE TIME FOR TEA?
UNCLE PHIL SAW YOU COMING THROUGH THE KITCHEN WINDOW!
MOM?... WHAT'S A FOGEY?
LYNN

IT WOULD BE NICE TO RUN AWAY FROM EVERY-THING FOR A WHILE.

YEAH.

WE COULD TAKE A MEDITERRANEAN CRUISE! NO HOUSE TO LOOK AFTER, NO COOKING, NO CLEAN-ING, NO KIDS....

WHOA!

SPA TREATMENTS, READING ON THE DECK... A COLD MARGARITA, SERVED BY A HANDSOME WAITER... SLEEPING LATE...

AAHHHH

MOM! COME QUICK!

IT'S HARD TO DREAM WHEN YOUR ALARM KEEPS GOING OFF!

FOR BETTER OR FOR WORSE
BY LYNN JOHNSTON

WHERE ARE YOU GOING, DADDY?

TO THE HARDWARE STORE.

I'M REALLY SORRY ABOUT THIS, JOHN.

DON'T WORRY ABOUT IT.

I KNOW IT'S ONLY A MINOR COMPLAINT.

IT'S OK.

MY WIFE WANTS ME TO RETURN THIS BATHTUB FAUCET AND SHOWER SET.

NOT QUITE RIGHT, EH?... WELL WHAT EXACTLY IS SHE LOOKING FOR?

... SOMETHING SHE CAN TURN OFF WITH HER FEET.

TUB FAUCET SET
TUB FAUCET SET
TUB FAUCET SET
TUB FAUCET SET
TUB FA

EARLY ARTISTIC INFLUENCES

While Lynn was growing up, there were no courses to take, no "how to" books, and no Saturday morning cartoon classes. Comic books, comic strip collections, "the funny pages," and the theatre were the resources of the 1950s and '60s. Budding cartoonists, storytellers, and comedians alike had to learn their craft gleaning ideas, tricks, and techniques anywhere and everywhere they could.

Lynn loved watching animated cartoons. Few people in her neighbourhood owned televisions, so in North Vancouver, the Odeon Theatre was the place to go. Each day, two feature films would be presented; between them ran the newsreel and at least three animated cartoons. For Lynn, good animation was often a bigger draw than the films they separated. Characters like Bugs Bunny, Daffy Duck, and Pepé Le Pew filled the screen with full-colour slapstick. For a dime, she would sit through the feature movies twice, so she could watch these entertaining cartoon characters come to life again and again. It was Lynn's father who really made her aware of the nuances of each character and how simple gestures could draw in the viewer — one glance could make or break a joke.

My dad loved slapstick. He taught us how to pratfall, to "wonky-walk," and to mime. He'd rent a movie projector and movies starring Charlie Chaplin, *Our Gang*, and the Keystone Kops. We didn't watch these films like an ordinary audience; we studied them. He would run scenes back and forth to show us how gags were set up, how everything was choreographed exactly to look spontaneous or to look like an accident.

My brother and I were soon aware of the way backgrounds repeated and how motion could be deliberately slowed down or sped up. He wanted us to see how comedy was created. If there was a formula to "funny," he wanted to find out what it was.

I played around with animation as soon as I had a school textbook in my hands. On the top right-hand corner of every page, I'd draw a stick figure, trying to make each one slightly different from the other. Walt Disney's weekly television show often gave us a behind-the-scenes look at the art of animation. We saw everything from the development of Mickey Mouse to how music and movement were synched together, so I knew I could make a character move if I could just draw enough pictures.

My dad and I never missed *Walt Disney*. The theme song still resonates in my head; I always thought it was Walt himself telling me to wish upon a star.

Lynn's father loved all forms of comedy, but he especially enjoyed comic art. Sitting with him and reading *Li'l Abner*, *Dick Tracy*, and *Peanuts*, Lynn learned to appreciate not just the artistry in comic art but also the structure of gags and the development of characters. Merv studied these drawings, and he taught his daughter to see the tiny details the cartoonists had injected into each panel.

By the age of ten, Lynn was a regular customer at her local second-hand bookstore, always on the lookout for cartoon books and comics that were new and different. She did read the superhero comics but had grown past them somehow.

I enjoyed the superhero stories, but they weren't funny. Even though I'd considered myself a superhero on the playground, fighting for the rights of the weak and downtrodden, I couldn't get into the world of super-fantasy. I scoffed at the female superheroes. Wonder Woman was just another wasp-waisted "Barbie," with big tits and no intellect. Catwoman was more of the same.

So often women in the comics were just decorations, meant to offset the dominant male. I couldn't picture myself hanging onto the ankle of some buffed-up poster boy crying, "Save me, Superguy! Save me!"

I liked the kind of cartoons that made me laugh, and to do that they had to be either slapstick, like Scrooge McDuck and company, or sophisticated, like Virgil Partch. (I looked for his work everywhere.)

Virgil Partch (or VIP) was known for his irreverent and often "sexy" subject matter. His booze-related gags were something Lynn's mother deemed inappropriate, which made his work all the more interesting. One year, Lynn saved up her allowance so she could buy one of Partch's books as a birthday gift for her father. She read the book carefully so it still looked new, gave it to her father, and then couldn't wait for Merv to finish reading it so she could read it again. She took it back to her room, where she read it over and over until the pages were worn and she had memorized his technique. His characteristic clean lines and fluid style were so enticing that Lynn began to copy his style.

What I loved was the way VIP drew profiles. He must have used a brush because his lines flowed thick and thin, and there was no way I could duplicate them with my mom's calligraphy pens, which I was using at the time. I loved his characters' large noses and protruding mouths. I loved the sarcastic expressions, the stocky bodies, and the simple backgrounds he drew. Everything in the picture was there for a purpose. VIP was an entirely different artist from what I was exposed to. The bawdiness of the subject matter appealed to me. He had an ability to "shock" the audience — just a little — using comedy. He was running a finger along the edge of adult humour without cutting into it. Anything my mom disapproved of appealed to me. I wanted to learn how to push the envelope, too. His work was a wonderful teaching resource for me.

Virgil Partch's office party scene from the book *VIP Tosses a Party*, 1959.

Len Norris, editorial cartoonist for the *Vancouver Sun*, was Lynn's father's favourite. Norris had a complex style that fascinated Lynn. She describes his work as "a delicious smorgasbord of hilarious detail." He had studied to be an architect, and every illustration exhibited his ability to draw in perspective with the most elegant line. His sense of humour extended well past the basic "gag," making each panel a treasure trove of minute comic nuances. Backgrounds were filled with funny elements, each one a gift to the reader, which made this artist's work significant and memorable. Lynn copied his work unabashedly, trying to learn how to make people laugh through line, detail, and dialogue.

"...They'll just have to make up their minds...trains running on time, or footling around in stations picking up passengers..."

Len Norris was able to demonstrate comic motion in a two-dimensional image.
His illustrations came to life and inspired Lynn to try to do the same.
From *The Best of Norris* (Toronto: McClelland and Stewart Ltd., 1984)

Len Norris taught me to give the audience more than they bargained for. Not only was he an astute political cartoonist, he was an observer of human nature. He included, wherever possible, elements we see around us but might not be aware of. I was impressed by his knowledge, his poignancy, and his reverence for life. He skewered upper crust snobs and unmasked political puppets more effectively than any columnist ever could. His work, his images, seared into my brain. When I look through the many Norris collection books, which I inherited from my dad, it amazes me that after forty years I still remember his cartoons as if I had read them yesterday.

Lynn illustrated a four-panel mural for a local Mexican restaurant.
The original panels were drawn in pen and coloured with Pantone markers,
circa 2005. The final mural was approximately three metres tall and over
nine metres long.

A number of other artists played major roles in the development of Lynn's drawing style, and in some cases, her storytelling as well. Charles Schulz's *Peanuts* was a newspaper comic strip she enjoyed, but her grandfather hated it. Lynn remembers he thought the dialogue was too mature: children couldn't possibly think or talk the way Charlie Brown and his friends did. Sitting next to her grandfather on his sofa as he read the "funnies" aloud, she listened to his critiques and heartily disagreed. She knew children were, indeed, sophisticated; they did have "adult" opinions, they just didn't have the maturity or the vocabulary to express them. Schulz's work, although it used adult vocabulary, appealed to children everywhere because it came from a child's point of view, and it did not condescend. Her grandfather's dismissal of this new and provocative strip made Charles Schulz one of Lynn's idols and "teachers." Lynn watched *Peanuts* evolve over the years, learning from the strip and being empowered by it.

This series of drawings demonstrates not only her love for Mexican culture but also her desire to bring an illustration to life and offer the viewer a comic journey while munching a burrito.

Both my dad and my grandfather analyzed the newspaper comics page. It intrigued me that these two learned people took the comics so seriously. My father liked to point out clever and unique details, which perhaps not every reader would notice. Gramps liked to tear things apart. He criticized the drawing. He said the characters in *Peanuts* and *Miss Peach* were distorted: the heads were too big and the backgrounds too sketchy. He preferred *Li'l Abner*, *Rex Morgan M.D.*, and *Dick Tracy*, which were realistically drawn and had believable storylines. Comics with rough doodles and cute gags he dismissed with a grunt... and yet he read them anyway. By listening to their "audience reaction," I was learning what worked and what didn't. I was also learning about sequence, timing, and dialogue.

A good example of an early strip that demonstrates Lynn's use of sequence and timing.

By the time Lynn entered high school, she was reading every publication she could find featuring cartoons. She had moved past comic books and was seeking out more "sophisticated stuff" — like the cartoons published in *Reader's Digest*, *The New Yorker*, and, when she could get her hands on one, *Playboy*.

Playboy cartoonists were [and still are] some of the best on the planet. I have been fortunate enough to have met several *Playboy* cartoonists and have seen their originals, which are larger than they appear in the magazine, and are spectacularly well done pieces of art. According to my friend Doug Sneyd (a *Playboy* cartoonist), Hugh Hefner loves comic art and has always given an entire page to his favourite cartoonists.

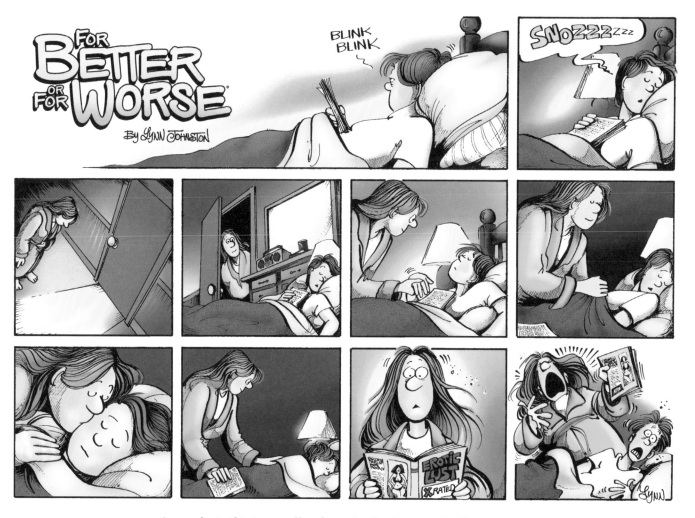

Lynn admits this is one of her favourite *For Better or For Worse* strips.

The New Yorker was where I found the most subtle and sophisticated humour. *The New Yorker* cartoonists engage the audience through a kind of intellectual "gotcha." I was hungry for the fast, sketch-like images, which showed a slice of life buttered with irony and embarrassing truths. When I found a whole collection of *New Yorker* cartoons in a huge coffee table–style book, I thought I'd discovered a gold mine! I knew then that I was going to work in this business. But how?

Jules Feiffer was one of the more sophisticated artists I studied. His work has appeared in *Playboy*, *The New Yorker*, and many other well-known publications. His intelligent and insightful prose taught me that good writing was the key to good comic art. One of Feiffer's most memorable characters, in my mind, was his Little Dancer. Drawn with just a few sketchy lines, this thin and forlorn little waif danced down the page as she opened her heart. She danced to art and to love, and to the folly of man. She was always worth "listening to," and as a young artist, she resonated with me.

I copied Jules Feiffer's dancer, and I tried to write her lines. I knew I was copying (something artists are severely criticized for doing), but I did so to learn. I never sold any of these drawings, but I did profit. Jules Feiffer was one of the teachers from whom I learned the art of writing relevant, yet entertaining, prose.

(above) Jules Feiffer's "Dancer" was a character he used time and again.
She always had a certain dishevelled look that Lynn loved.

(below) Lynn has adopted some of Feiffer's style when it comes to movement and "female curves."

Lynn always enjoyed drawing Elly as a frazzled, frumpy housewife. Perhaps this is a reflection of her own emotions, or perhaps it is a nod to her hero, Jules Feiffer.

It was the 1960s, a period that experienced a renaissance in just about everything. The Vietnam War had exhausted and overwhelmed two generations. People broke from tradition and the dominant culture any way they could. *Irreverent* was the watchword of the decade. With her mother's conservative admonishments ringing in her ears, Lynn and her contemporaries were keener than ever to explore the arts — to see what was "out there."

Like everyone else my age, I wanted to break free and express myself. I just didn't know how! I took my guitar to coffee houses and tried to emulate Joan Baez. I was awful. I made goofy movies with friends who'd scored their dad's Bolex camera, and I wrote long, tedious poems about angst and longing — wanting it to sound like the work of Jules Feiffer (his monologues were a wonderful discovery). I tried a lot of things, but always ended up back at the drawing board. The one thing I could do was draw, but there was nothing out there that really inspired me to draw. And then, I discovered *MAD*!

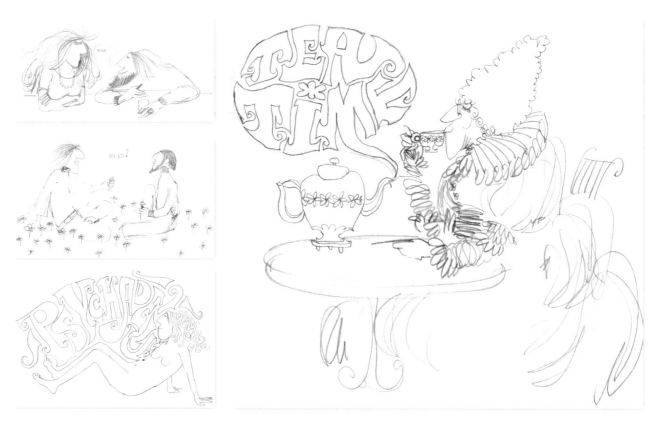

A few examples of Lynn's "hippy" art and the influence the 1960s had on her early work.

MAD magazine debuted in the United States in 1952, when Lynn was only five years old, but she didn't see her first copy until she was in her early teens. By the time it reached North Vancouver, its youthful, twisted satire had set the world of comic art on fire. In Lynn's opinion, MAD had the most outstanding, creative talent ever assembled.

My mother thought it was crude and offensive: "It's disgusting, dear," she would say. "I don't want you looking at all those awful illustrations and reading that . . . *stuff*!" If Mom found me reading Virgil Partch, she'd take the book away because it was Dad's, but if she saw a MAD magazine in the house, she'd destroy it. This made MAD even more wonderful! My friends and I would buy MAD and then pass it around, hidden in something like *Little Lulu* or *Mickey Mouse*. We'd remove the cover of an acceptable comic and fit the MAD inside. I would disappear into the alcove under the basement stairs and read the contraband, loving every part of it and trying not to laugh out loud. I began to copy from MAD as I'd done from Norris and VIP, learning what I could from the artists whose work I so admired.

MAD's artists became the new go-to guys if you wanted to be a cartoonist. Don Martin's super goofy characters and so-dumb-they-were-funny gags inspired copycats and wannabes, while Al Jaffee's fold-ins made illustration and satire history. With Mort Drucker's caricatures and *Spy vs. Spy* vying for top comic art billing, *MAD* magazine was the best possible resource there was for those of us bent on a career in the comics.

This is from the book cover of a *MAD* collection that exclusively featured Jaffee's fold-ins. Lynn provided a quote for the book's inside cover: "Like Al himself, his work is one-of-a-kind."
From Al Jaffee, *MAD Fold This Book!* (New York, NY: Warner Treasures, 1997)
™ & © E.C. Publications, Inc.

One *MAD* cartoonist who strongly inspired Lynn was Sergio Aragonés. Born in Spain, Aragonés moved to the United States from Mexico in the early '60s. He was hired by *MAD* to do something other than gag-based, panel cartoons. He solidified his career at *MAD* with his prolific nature and his ability to draw simple dialogue-free gags in the empty spaces around the other cartoons on the page — known as "marginals." It is his ultra-clever use of the margins of *MAD*, his burlesque style, and his rapid-fire imagery that delight readers and cartoonists everywhere — in any language.

His art draws you in — it's friendly and funny. Most of Sergio's cartoons are done in pantomime, and in cartooning less is more. It's about getting to the essence of the gag. [...] To be able to tell a joke with funny drawings alone is a pure form of communication, and to do this well is extremely difficult. [...] Like the great "silent" film comedians — Chaplin, Keaton, Tati — Sergio makes it look easy. His work is deceptive in its simplicity.

I remember, I remember,
That bleary, bombed-out mass
That wandered 'round the countryside
Freaked out on hash and grass;
Not all of them, I wish to say,
Possessed a glassy stare;
A few, in fact, could still recall
The reason they were there!

Woodstock, with text by Frank Jacobs, is of one of thousands of complex illustrations that Sergio Aragonés has drawn over the years.
From *MAD* #263 © E.C. Publications, Inc.

It is difficult to look at Aragonés's work and not be inspired. No image goes to waste — every illustration and every incidental character is there for a purpose. Each bit player is doing, saying, or thinking something that adds value to the narrative.

One thing that always impresses me about Sergio's work is his constant comedy. I learned to extend the visual life of my cartoons by making every character in a scene have a role to play — without overwhelming the gag. It's like directing a film, in a way. Sergio acts out every part: from the guy at centre stage to the lowly looker-on. He uses all of his "actors," gives them character and personality, without overwhelming the star. Sergio breathes life into a scene — just as Len Norris, Al Jaffee and VIP had done. From the day I first read *MAD* magazine, Sergio became another one of my teachers.

Lynn adopted Aragonés's marginal style for her high school annual when she filled in the empty spaces of the sports section with these fun characters. There are also signs of VIP's, Norris's, and Feiffer's influence.
("Norseman," North Vancouver Senior Secondary School Annual, 1964)

So many cartoonists and creators have influenced Lynn and helped her to develop her drawing and writing style — it is difficult to mention them all. On occasion Lynn has been asked to teach drawing classes for students who are serious about cartooning. One question she is often asked is whether or not it is OK to copy another artist's work.

My advice is to tell them, yes, its OK to copy another artist's work, as long as you're just trying to learn something and not trying to profit from it. No professional artist with pride and decency will knowingly duplicate another artist's style. I think we all incorporate minute details — nuances, if you will — of the work which influenced us most. It is nearly impossible not to.

CREATIVE, HARDWORKING, AND CONFIDENT: NOW WHAT?

Lynn graduated from high school in 1965. Like almost every student who is forced out into the real world, Lynn had difficulty choosing a career path. She recalls she was never good in math, and academia didn't appeal to her. She knew she was good at art. Her involvement in creating her high school annual was the experience that set the stage for her future as a professional graphic artist.

Lynn at age eighteen.

In high school I was privileged to work with teachers who could see my potential, and they began to give me challenges. I created posters for school events, illustrated pamphlets and memos, and with each completed task, another project would be assigned. At one point, I was asked to do illustrations for the school annual. When I saw that the layout could be improved, I became a regular member of the annual committee. By grade eleven, I was the editor — I was in charge of the whole book. I discovered that working with a creative team of students, people who actually did their jobs with confidence and pride, was a profound and joyful experience. The teaching staff treated this team like adults. For me, this changed everything. I began to see myself as a graphic artist who could take on a complex project — and make it happen.

Lynn drew this heading page for
her high school annual.
("Norseman," North Vancouver Senior
Secondary School Annual, 1964)

It was one of Lynn's teachers who recommended her to the director of the Vancouver School of Art (VSA). Each year, a small number of exceptional students were chosen from schools all over the Vancouver area to attend VSA. She submitted a portfolio, and it was accepted. For the first time, Lynn was in an environment entirely devoted to drawing, painting, and self-expression. To be studying art seriously, after all this time, was an electrifying experience.

> Evenings, weekends, and after school, we learned anatomy, history,
> and life drawing. The shock of seeing the first nude model quickly
> disappeared as I concentrated on position, perspective, and form.

In her first year, the students were introduced to everything from pottery to painting to graphic design. Lynn remembers there was much camaraderie amongst the students — for the first time, they were in an environment where artists were not teased or criticized for being a little "different." And for the first time, Lynn was with other artists much like herself.

J. Ridgway '64

Lynn's sketch drawn from a live model at the Vancouver School of Art, 1964.

The Vancouver School of Art was a fine arts college. By second year it was evident to me that I was gravitating toward a rather motley little group of commercial illustrators and breaking away from the realists, the impressionists, and the gallery crowd. My inability to take things seriously had haunted me all through elementary and high school and was again overshadowing my work. I turned my polar bear sculpture into an aircraft because its nose resembled a Cessna, I glued wire wool to the armpits of my "bust of woman." Perfect renderings of the class skeleton were done of him leaning against a bar smoking cigarettes. My portrait of "a nude, scratching" did not win points. I moved from the fashionable "in" crowd of abstract expressionists and producers of contemporary art into the realm of commercial illustrators. Commercial art, as some saw it, was the bottom of the barrel. Only hacks, people who wanted to do art for a living went that route, and the school, it seemed, was ill-equipped to train us at the time. Color was now the norm in magazines. It was rumored that newspapers would be able to reproduce photographs with four-color plates; television had made an immense impact on the advertising industry; and here we were rendering black-and-white tuna casseroles with smudged chalk and frisket paper. Despite whatever grumbling I may have done, I learned, my work improved, and I had the opportunity to try my skills in a number of mediums.

Lynn worked in various mediums at VSA, including macramé!

While in art school, Lynn had been working part-time in her father's jewellery store. Here she met Ken Walker, who happened to be the manager of Canawest Films. Lynn babysat for his family a number of times. Through this job, Walker became familiar with Lynn's work, and he was aware of her frustrations at art school. Knowing she was interested in animation, he gave her several reels of "black leader," the black film used to thread a movie into a projector. He showed her how to scratch into it with a stylus so that when the leader was run through a projector, the scratches would move just like animated images. With a sharp knife and felt pens, Lynn worked for hours on the black film. At twenty-four frames per second, images had to be drawn hundreds of times in miniature between the sprockets.

Lynn recalls she managed to create some interesting fast-paced animation, much like the work of famed National Film Board artist Norman McLaren. Walker was impressed. He suggested she apply for a summer job at Canawest Films. They had just signed a contract and were about to do some "piece work" on a series of animated shows. In the summer between her second and third year, here was an opportunity to work in a real animation studio; she couldn't pass it up.

> I was hired one summer to work for Canawest Films, a studio that
> did commercials and segments of Saturday morning cartoons such
> as *Abbott and Costello* and *Shazzan*. These were Hanna-Barbera
> productions, and the Vancouver staff was pressured to churn out
> as many shows as possible, as fast as possible. We worked a grueling
> schedule to keep production going for 24 hours a day. I was in the ink
> and paint department (something that doesn't really exist anymore),
> and although the job was tiresome and repetitive, I learned more about
> animation than I could through any course. By the end of the summer,
> I had decided that I wanted a career as an animator.

"LOU COSTELLO" - BP-SERIES:

©HANNA-BARBERA PRODUCTIONS, INC.
1966

At Canawest Films, Lynn picked up off the floor this unfinished character sheet of Lou Costello from Hanna-Barbera's *Abbott and Costello*. Thousands of these were thrown away; many ended up in landfills.

This meant dropping out of art school. To this day, however, she regrets that she never completed her schooling at VSA.

One of the best things to come from Lynn's time at Canawest was her lifelong friendship with fellow cartoonist and illustrator Cecily Sell, from Los Angeles. She was newly wed to a Canadian and had moved to Vancouver to be with her husband, who worked at a local radio station. Lynn was also newly married, having wed in 1967. She'd met her husband, Doug Franks, through mutual friends in broadcasting; he worked as a television cameraman. Lynn and Cecily shared a love of comic art, and both lived with ambitious men whose fields were fiercely competitive, which would prove a deterrent to Lynn's and Cecily's opportunities in animation.

(left) In the dining room of Lynn's parents' house on 5th Street in North Vancouver, Lynn and Doug cut the cake at their 1967 wedding ceremony. Lynn had just turned twenty.

(right) Doodle of Lynn and Doug, 1969.

Canawest was coming to the end of their contract with Hanna-Barbera. There was also a rumour that Doug's job at the CBC (Canadian Broadcasting Corporation) might become part-time. With nothing to lose, the two couples decided to drive to Los Angeles to visit Cecily's parents, Alpine and Cecil Beard — they "knew all kinds of people in the animation and film industry and were willing to make some connections for us."

Lynn recalls Alpine and Cecil Beard as charming comic characters. Alpine was talkative, open, and oblivious to the chaos around her. Cecil, who spoke with a thick Texas accent and sported a white Santa beard, was gregarious, theatrical, and kind. He had worked for many years for Disney as an animator on great projects such as *Fantasia*, where his ability to animate crashing waves and rushing water gained him admiration in an era when everything was done by hand. Once retired, Alpine and Cecil wrote stories for comic books such as *Scrooge McDuck* and *Gyro Gearloose*. Lynn notes that Alpine wrote under Cecil's name because, at the time, Disney Studios refused to buy anything written by a woman: "Cecil turned in an enormous amount of work, and Disney just thought that he was incredibly prolific."

Through Cecily's well-connected parents, she and Lynn were given an opportunity to show their portfolios at Jay Ward Studios. Lynn remembers it was located in a funny little building on Sunset Strip and was known as the best and most innovative animation studio in Los Angeles. They presented their folios and were both immediately offered jobs in the backgrounds department — to start as soon as possible.

(right) Cecily and Lynn, near Cecily's home in Seattle, WA, 2005.

(below) Lynn and Cecily lost touch once Lynn moved to Ontario. They reconnected when Lynn, trying to find her friend, put her name into the comic strip, and they have remained close ever since.

Jay Ward was famous for *George of the Jungle*, *Rocky and Bullwinkle*, and my personal fave, *Super Chicken*! All I had to do was get a Green card, Cecily could move home, and the guys could find something, we were sure! Not so. Radio announcers and television cameramen were everywhere in California. There was no need to hire from out of the country. Both men refused to take "just anything" so their wives could become animators. The four of us drove back to Vancouver. This was heart breaking, but we followed our men.

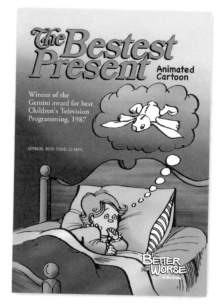

DVD cover of *The Bestest Present* made-for-television program.

Of course, Lynn didn't realize at the time that she would eventually fulfill her desire to animate when she ventured into animation with her own characters. Lynn produced a number of animated *For Better or For Worse* specials over the years. Of them all, *The Bestest Present* has been the most successful and well received.

ONE OPEN DOOR LEADS TO ANOTHER

Shortly after the trip to Los Angeles, Doug lost his job at the CBC to spending cutbacks. The prospects in Vancouver were bleak, so he left for Ontario, where work in his field was more readily available. He landed a job at CHCH TV in Hamilton, a steel town on the shore of Lake Ontario. "We made plans to go east, just for a while, to find temporary work. When the situation improved, we'd go back to Vancouver."

Lynn would have liked to continue her apprenticeship, but there were no animation studios in Hamilton. There were a few in Toronto, but distance was not her only obstacle; she didn't have the proper training or the equipment to take on freelance work yet.

At the time I was learning how to animate, busy animation studios would farm out shows, or even parts of shows, to smaller, satellite studios. A studio in Toronto might get a contract to do part of a show for Hanna-Barbera, for example. This could be a storyboard, just the backgrounds, or a few specific scenes from one show. Several animators could work on one scene, which then allowed some experienced animators to work from home.

New to town and in debt from the move, Lynn had to find another kind of job. Believing their stint in Hamilton was going to be short-lived, she went door-to-door, applying to shops and restaurants. Lynn was on the verge of abandoning "any hope of resuming an artistic career when an ad in the *Hamilton Spectator* leapt off the page, so to speak. Hamilton General Hospital needed a graphic artist, someone who could do charts and graphs for medical students." Naturally, she seized the opportunity.

I called the number and made an appointment with the head of photography. I then worked all day and into the night making a folio that showed I could do charts, graphs, guts, bones — whatever I thought they'd want to see. This was a good thing. I'd have never been offered the job if all he'd seen was cartoons!

(above) Lynn drew this piece for a talk, with slides, about hospital administration and how those taking notes were often left to do the entire job, resulting in frustration and errors.

(below) Lynn got used to rejection during her early days in Hamilton.

By noon the following day, Lynn had been hired by the head of photography for the Hamilton General Hospital to do, well, she wasn't quite sure what.

Lynn describes the space she was given as a narrow utility room in the basement with a small, barred window facing a wall. It was two doors down from the morgue, where the hum of the ventilation, high-pitched saws, and muffled conversation filled the air. Her first assignment was surprisingly grim.

> As soon as I arrived, I was asked to sit with a young mother who had been beaten by her husband. She had to have her wounds photographed as evidence against him. I was as embarrassed as she was. They had to light the bruises so they could be clearly seen in the photographs. I held back her hair so lacerations on her head were visible. I moved her gown to cover her while the bruising on her back was photographed, and I held her baby when she wasn't able to. I felt awful about this, but after a couple of similar scenarios, I knew this was more of a comfort to the women than an intrusion on their privacy. I think I was actually hired because they needed a female present when they photographed women.

Lynn was asked to do a few charts and graphs, as well as other random jobs, but it wasn't enough to fill her time, and soon she was at loose ends. Bored and curious, she wandered around the hospital looking for more to do.

> I had befriended one of the nurses in radiology. I asked if I could look around her department. This is where I met Dr. Harald Stolberg, who was the head of radiology. He specialized in the workings of the heart and was about to go to Germany to give a series of lectures. I was asked if I knew how to operate a rotoscope. I did.
>
> A rotoscope is a projector that shoots an image up from the floor-level onto a frosted surface allowing an artist to trace the images one at a time for accuracy and effect. It's like seeing a movie from behind the screen. At the time, this machine was used by animators in order to draw a perfect walk cycle of an animal, for example. I had become familiar with the rotoscope while working at Canawest Films.

Dr. Stolberg was using this device to trace angiogram images, which he would use to illustrate his lectures. Once he learned Lynn was capable of operating the rotoscope, she was immediately taken to a small room near his office, given a pen, some acetate, and a fast lecture on constrictions of the circumflex artery.

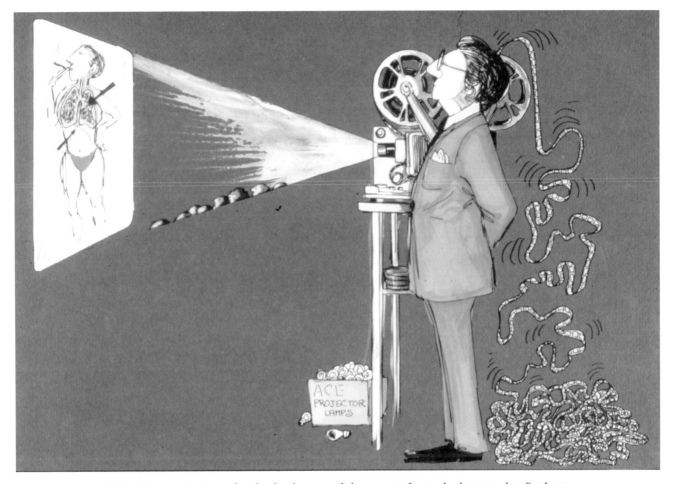

The 16mm projectors often broke down, and there was often nobody around to fix them.

I was left to do the job the best I could do. For the next few weeks, I worked on Harald Stolberg's illustrations in my free time, learning as I went along. It was fascinating and frustrating at the same time. I was not a medical illustrator, and here I was doing some very technical illustrations.

The relationship Lynn built with Dr. Stolberg and his staff did not sit well with the head of photography — her boss. He felt she had overstepped her boundaries by working in another department on "his time." Lynn was still within her six-month probation period before her employment was secured.

Dr. Paul Potter shows Lynn how to use a high-intensity microscope, 1969.

So with only a few weeks left to go, I was fired for "inadequate ability."
[…] When I told Dr. Stolberg I was unable to complete his illustrations,
he was furious. He picked up his phone, called down to photography,
and shouted so hard that his dentures flew out!

The following day, he suggested I meet Dr. Cockshott, the head of
radiology at McMaster University. A new and revolutionary teaching
hospital was being built, and he was looking for artists who could
illustrate lectures for a select group of medical students. Professors
were looking for innovative ways to deliver lectures and other
information to their students in a visually interesting and easily
accessible way. I was recommended by Dr. Stolberg. After about a
week of unemployment, I was hired. I'd been given a second chance.

While the new hospital was under construction, the university rented a space in the Chedoke
Hospital. Here they assembled a select group of people who would be working for McMaster
University Medical Centre (MUMC, or "MUMSY" as it was affectionately called). Artists, students,
teachers, doctors, anatomists, and technicians (prosectors) all worked together in tight quarters.

Pioneers ourselves in the new program, Paul [Lynn's supervisor] and I
began to work with the medical teaching staff. We produced, at first, dry,
wordy visual lectures — white lettering on blue diazo slides; slide after
slide after chart after boring graph. Several doctors, discovering that
we could actually *draw*, began to give us more challenging illustrations,
and one suggested that we both be trained more as medical illustrators
than as graphic artists. We were accepted as part of the "team" of young,
first year students; we attended lectures, went on rounds, watched and
participated in dissections, observed animal experiments, and were
treated with great consideration. It was to be the best job I would ever
have in my life … as nine to five jobs go!

Lynn's drawing depicts the frustrating situation in the radiology department: there was too much material to store and no space to store it, 1969.

ESOPHAGEAL VARICES GASTRIC ULCER

Lynn and her fellow artists were asked to devise a method to illustrate an organ with varying forms or stages of disease, without having to draw the same organ over and over again. Surprisingly, animation cels provided the answer: the healthy organ was drawn on card stock in full colour, then an illustration of the desired abnormality was made on clear acetate film and placed over the original image. Animation ink and paint became invaluable tools of the trade; hundreds of medical illustrations were created using this technique.

Lynn found the work at McMaster University diverse and challenging. It offered her a valuable education in anatomy and the medical field — a field she never would have expected to be in.

Lynn's painting style is already recognizable in this early example of her medical art.

UNFAZED BY THEIR SURROUNDINGS ... "THE UNCLENCHABLES" CAME TO EAT LUNCH IN THE ONLY ROOM IN THE BUILDING THAT WAS AIR CONDITIONED.

Lynn and her co-workers often ate lunch in the dissection lab in the basement
of Chedoke Hospital. It was the only air-conditioned room.
This group became known as the "Unclenchables."

Aside from the medical materials they were usually asked to produce, it wasn't uncommon for Lynn and the other medical artists in the department to be given seemingly mundane tasks, such as drawing up invitations or advertisements for dances and other events or enhancing slide presentations.

Medical school is a stream of symbols, signs, compounds, diagrams, measurements, and unending facts to be understood and memorized. It was our job to make these facts easier to retain. It was the brainchild of one researcher to have us do cartoons to help break the monotony. Having seen some of my less than reverent drawings, David Sackett asked me to work with him on a project about wind- and water-borne bacteria and how they affect the health of people in rural areas. The result was a slide presentation done entirely with cartoons.

A sample of a sketch Lynn was asked to produce for a staff Christmas greeting card, 1972.

Sackett's classes and presentations were hugely popular, and soon Lynn was drawing, almost exclusively, cartoons for the university. Lynn recalls some of the more traditional-minded professors were surprised that students were retaining information from the cartoon diagrams far better than they were from the standard visual aids.

Once the new teaching hospital was completed and everyone was settled into their appropriate departments, Lynn observed the politics of the school destroy the exciting and dynamic atmosphere that had developed at the temporary location. There were now supervisors supervising supervisors, and in order for Lynn to even talk to certain individuals, she would have to go through "appropriate channels." Relationships became difficult to maintain. McMaster University Medical Centre gained worldwide recognition for its new and innovative teaching facility, but for Lynn, her job there had lost its lustre.

Examples of slides Lynn produced
to accompany medical lectures.

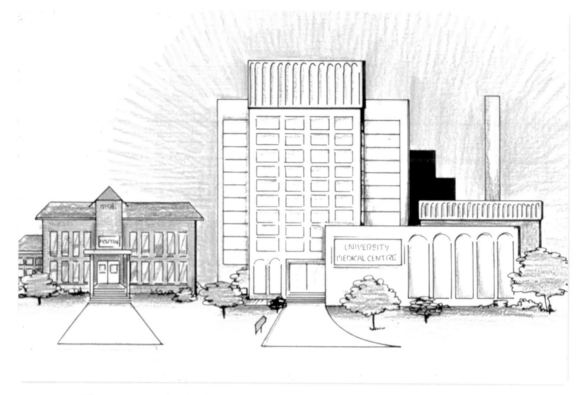

This was not a sketch of McMaster, just an example of how things were changing.
Lynn illustrates the way new, modern buildings were taking the place
of the rustic, smaller ones — efficiency over charm.

One person whom Lynn had befriended at this site would prove to be a true friend for life. Marjorie Baskin worked in public relations. Lynn describes her as direct, outspoken, and demanding but a remarkable advocate for Lynn.

I loved working for Marjorie. If I did work that was not acceptable, she let me know. If I did work that was outstanding, she praised me to the stars — something that I was not accustomed to. Marjorie taught me to do the best I could possibly do, at all times, and to always do work I was proud of, to get it in on time, and to be willing to take constructive criticism. It's hard to accept someone else's direction if you think you are right, if you think you're exceptional. She took me down a few pegs when I needed it most. After a year on the job, I was beginning to think I was a gift to the university. Of all of the people I worked for at McMaster, I worked the hardest for Marjorie — just as I had for my school teachers who were tough but fair. I needed her praise, and I needed her friendship.

SHE'S RUNNING AGAIN!

Part of a brochure Lynn created for Marjorie Baskin
for a Board of Education campaign, 1975.

68

Outside of work, Marjorie became a sort of surrogate mother to Lynn. She offered guidance and a perspective on life that Lynn acknowledges she really needed at the time. They would remain very close friends until Marjorie passed away in 2005.

While Lynn was enjoying her job and her friendships at McMaster, her relationship with Doug was getting rocky. Despite the arguments and the frustration, Lynn did her best to keep the marriage together.

Lynn at work in her converted greenhouse studio.

By now we were too entrenched in the east to return to Vancouver. We bought a small house in Dundas overlooking a pretty ravine. In the evenings, I did freelance work from a greenhouse we turned into a studio. We fought, made up, and fought again.

Occasionally on the weekends, Lynn and Doug would go on road trips to get away from everyday stresses. One weekend they visited Walsingham, Ontario, wondering what there was to do. A sign in the corner store read, "Old English Sheepdog Puppies For Sale." With nothing better to do, they set off to see what the puppies looked like.

The address took us to a rural farmhouse. The latest litter was ready to go. We had no intention of buying a dog. We'd just moved into our first house, we had full-time jobs, and we enjoyed our freedom. Still, Doug grew up with a dog, so before we knew it, we were writing a cheque and bundling this funny, squirmy pup into a cardboard box and taking him home. We named the puppy "Farley" after Farley Mowat, the author.

A caricature of Farley Mowat by Lynn that was used to promote a newly published collection of Mowat's stories at a bookstore in Burlington, Ontario.

I had met Farley several times at the Different Drummer bookstore in Burlington. Like many independents, the Different Drummer provided exceptional opportunities for readers to hear their favourite authors speak and to meet them afterward. I did many illustrations for this lively and innovative shop, and when I was asked to draw caricatures of Farley Mowat, I was thrilled. I was able to get to know him personally, and it gave me great pleasure when he later accepted my original Farley comic strips as gifts.

Farley (the puppy) gave Lynn and Doug something to do together, and because of him, their relationship improved.

We both adored the dog, but as the dog grew, he became an arduous task; he shed everywhere, was hard to train, and needed a great deal of attention. After a while, he became *my* responsibility, which was OK. He was funny and fun and good company when I was alone in the house — which was often.

Farley the dog was, of course, the inspiration behind the most popular and most loveable character in *For Better or For Worse*.

One of the few images of Lynn with Farley as a puppy, 1972.
They are posing behind her house in Dundas, above the ravine
in the backyard, the same ravine that the character
Farley would later rescue April from.

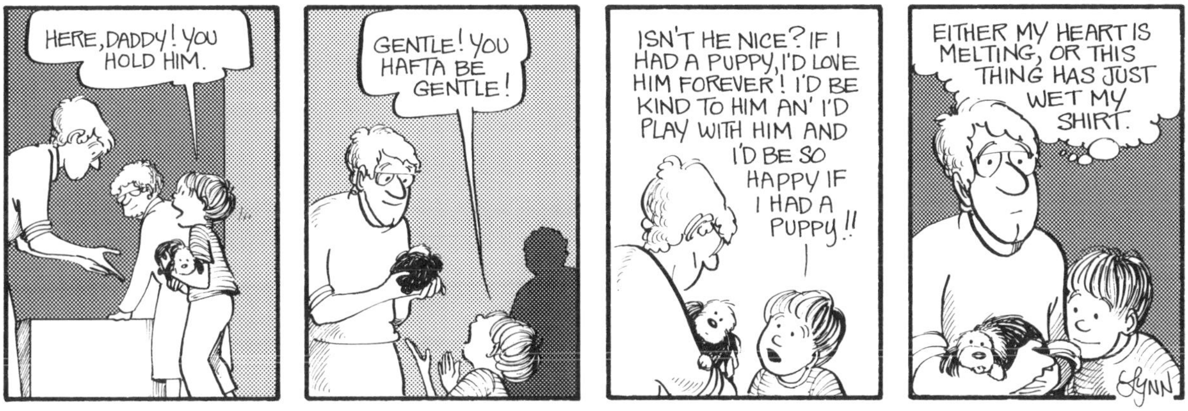
HERE, DADDY! YOU HOLD HIM.
GENTLE! YOU HAFTA BE GENTLE!
ISN'T HE NICE? IF I HAD A PUPPY, I'D LOVE HIM FOREVER! I'D BE KIND TO HIM AN' I'D PLAY WITH HIM AND I'D BE SO HAPPY IF I HAD A PUPPY!!
EITHER MY HEART IS MELTING, OR THIS THING HAS JUST WET MY SHIRT.
LYNN

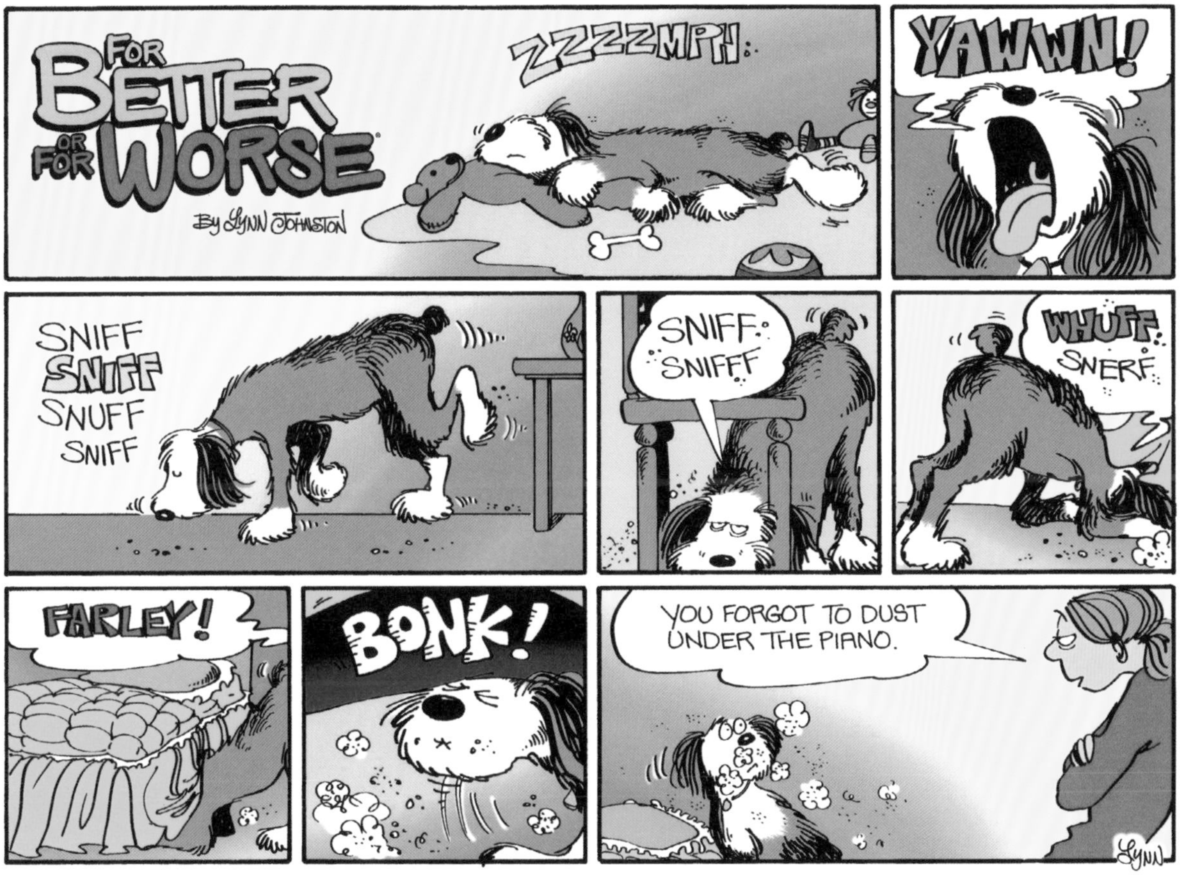
FOR BETTER OR FOR WORSE
BY LYNN JOHNSTON
ZZZZMPH
YAWWN!
SNIFF
SNIFF
SNUFF
SNIFF
SNIFF SNIFFF
WHUFF SNERF
FARLEY!
BONK!
YOU FORGOT TO DUST UNDER THE PIANO.
LYNN

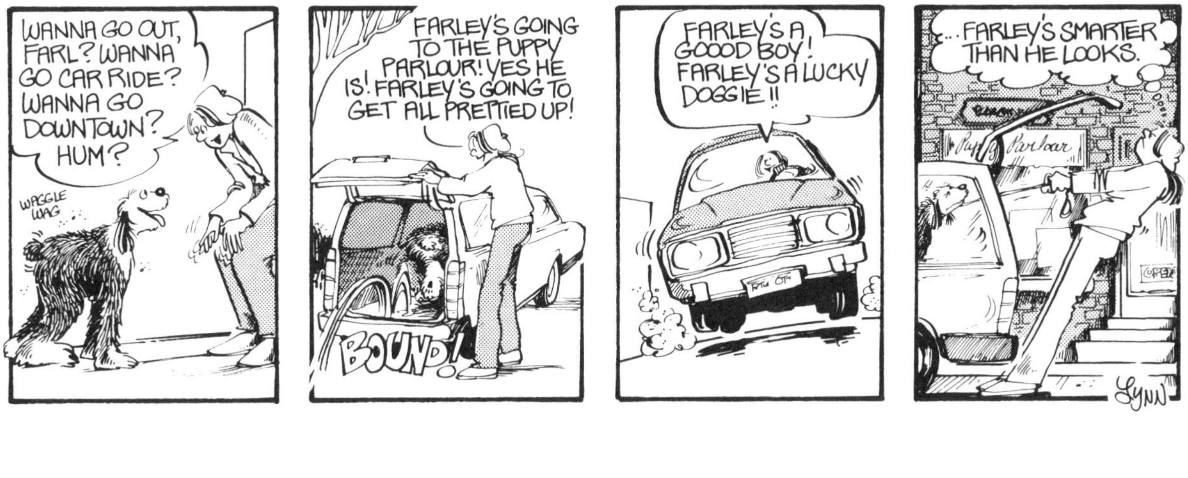
WANNA GO OUT, FARL? WANNA GO CAR RIDE? WANNA GO DOWNTOWN? HUM?
WAGGLE WAG
FARLEY'S GOING TO THE PUPPY PARLOUR! YES HE IS! FARLEY'S GOING TO GET ALL PRETTIED UP!
BOUND!
FARLEY'S A GOOOD BOY! FARLEY'S A LUCKY DOGGIE!!
...FARLEY'S SMARTER THAN HE LOOKS.
LYNN

Outside of her full-time job at McMaster Lynn was building a growing number of freelance clients for whom she did advertisements, illustrations, and other design work. When she wasn't doing work for hire, she submitted cartoons to the *Dundas Valley Journal*.

She wrote long letters home to her parents, illustrated with cartoons of life in Dundas, and practised the guitar. Lynn spent a lot of time hanging out at the studios where Doug was working and pitched in whenever they needed an extra pair of hands. (This was before union rules made it impossible for anyone outside a particular position to touch the props or move a camera.) One of the "props guys" there at the time was Rod Johnston, a talkative character who set up backdrops, fixed puppets, moved furniture, and did whatever else was necessary to create a stage in the studio. Lynn admits she liked him and enjoyed seeing him whenever she was there.

The new teaching system at the medical centre was excelling; some of the teaching-aid techniques Lynn had helped to develop were gaining popularity, and more and more professors were asking for graphic art to accompany their lectures. New people were hired to help keep

Samples of Lynn's cartoons published in the *Dundas Valley Journal*.

up the pace, and Lynn began to feel herself breaking away. She was twenty-six by now and was starting to think about having a family. And her freelance work was steady enough that she was prepared to establish a small business at home.

The subject of having a baby drove a wedge between Lynn and Doug. She desperately wanted a child, and he wavered. He eventually left the decision entirely up to Lynn, who chose to let providence take over.

Our relationship was deteriorating rapidly. We had been fighting about Doug's frequent absences. After work, he would go to a bar, and if he wasn't home for dinner, I knew he might not come home all night. One night I decided to leave. I began to pack my bags. If he didn't come home by the time I was packed and ready, then I'd get a cab to the airport and buy a ticket to Vancouver. I had had enough. I packed everything I could

Lynn's comic often touched on the theme of shifting gender roles, especially in the '80s when "working moms" were a fairly new phenomenon.

into two suitcases, took a cab to the Toronto airport, and bought a one-way ticket to Vancouver. It was a decision that had been long overdue. I was so upset that I left without telling a soul. As much as I hated to, I left behind my dog, too.

In a fog of panic and despair, I arrived at my parents' home and was ushered to my childhood bedroom. It hadn't changed. It was surreal. I lay in my bed thinking, "I had a house, a job I loved, friends, and a dog. What am I doing here?!" My parents were non-judgmental. They welcomed me home, but my problems were mine to solve. They offered no assistance and no advice. They offered to let me stay with them while I got on my feet.

I immediately set off to find employment and a place to live. Within a couple of days, I found an apartment, but it wasn't going to be available

Lynn still loves a good furniture shop.

for two weeks. With furnishing it in mind, I went into a furniture store and was so enthusiastic about their merchandise, I told them I could sell it! I said I'd been a sales clerk for my dad, which was true. The manager knew my dad and offered me a job. The job was to start at the end of the month — the same time my apartment would be available.

With two weeks to kill before her new independence began, Lynn decided to look up an old friend from art school who was living in a remote area of the province on the side of a mountain, high above Seton Portage. To visit Bernhard Thor meant taking the PGE (Pacific Great Eastern) Railway, which was running passengers into the province's interior at the time, to an uninhabited location along the rail. From there, the remainder of the journey had to be made on horseback. Lynn would be seeing an area her Aunt Unity loved and had documented in paintings and sketches.

I was let out of the train on the tracks in the middle of nowhere — below the "string bag post," which held the mail. Out of the brush, whooping and hollering, came my friend, Bernhard, riding one horse and leading another. He loaded up my luggage onto one horse and helped me onto the other. We rode together up into the wildest, most spectacular mountain country I'd ever seen.

Bernhard lived alone at the time. I had a room to myself in his hobbit-like cabin, which he had built himself. It was a memorable home to say the least. Walls, doorways, and windows were adorned with twisted woodcarvings, his stairs were sculpted from stone. I felt welcome, and more than anything, I felt loved — true platonic love. With his kindness and affection, I began to recover from my broken marriage and fast exodus from Ontario. A week into my visit, I began to feel ill. Having fathered two sons himself, Bernhard diagnosed my illness as pregnancy. He asked me to stay, but I needed to go back to North Vancouver and see my doctor. I promised I'd return. I did, but not for many years.

Bernhard Thor and Lynn are still close friends. Lynn photographed him in front of the entrance to his secluded home, 2007.

Lynn expressed her own anxieties about parenthood through cartooning.

With my pregnancy confirmed, I was left to consider my options.
My parents were of no help. They decided to go to their cottage to give
me time and space, to be alone with my thoughts. In the meantime,
without my knowledge, Doug had arrived in Vancouver. We had a long
talk. He promised to settle down and do his best to be a good father,
and so I agreed to move back to Ontario with him. It was a calculated
risk. If things turned out well, then my marriage would be saved. If he
continued his old habits, then I'd break away from him, but I'd have the
baby and the house — things I had been wanting for so long.

Lynn, shortly before Aaron's birth, at home in
Dundas with Farley at her feet, 1973.

Back in Ontario, life became positive. Lynn tried to get her job back
at McMaster. By leaving her job unannounced, understandably, they
had hired someone else. Luckily, she had retained most of her freelance
clients. With some effort, she managed to secure enough work to keep
herself employed.

Marjorie Baskin continued to hire Lynn to do occasional work for the
hospital, as did some of the doctors. Among these was Dr. Murray Enkin,
a well-respected obstetrician who had asked Lynn to draw a special
series of cartoons for him. He wished to illustrate, in a humorous way,
the exercises he recommended to his pregnant patients — the Lamaze

and Leboyer methods. It was because of her good relationship with Dr. Enkin that he accepted her as a patient, even though he specialized in difficult pregnancies. One of the first obstetricians to promote natural childbirth, Lynn recalls his office was full of posters about awareness, choice options, and family involvement.

I loved working for Murray. He appreciated the work I did, and he treated me like an equal. He has played a pivotal role in my life. Innovative, outgoing, brilliant, and fun, his friendship gave me strength and encouragement. As a pregnant patient, I often lay half-dressed on a gurney waiting for examination. Nine months of regular visits to his clinic made me familiar with the staff and the surroundings. One day I complained that there was nothing to look at during the examinations, and why didn't they put something on the ceiling?

Murray's response was, "You're the cartoonist. I challenge you to draw something for my ceiling." This was all the incentive I needed.

Lynn enjoyed documenting the absurd elements of pregnancy.

WELL, WELL, THERE YOU ARE! SORRY TO KEEP YOU WAITING.

EVERYTHING LOOKS OK AND SOUNDS OK...

I'D SAY BABY IS HEALTHY AND DEVELOPING NORMALLY, MRS. PATTERSON. — IS THERE ANYTHING YOU'D LIKE TO ASK BEFORE I GO?

YES...

... HOW LONG HAS IT BEEN SINCE YOU PAINTED YOUR CEILING?

Sometimes a punchline would remain in reserve for decades before Lynn was able to use it.

Lynn began to draw cartoons for Dr. Enkin's examining-room ceiling. She poured her thoughts and ideas, her frustrations and her fears about pregnancy into these simple, single-panel, roughly drawn cartoons. She would present Dr. Enkin with another handful of drawings each time she had an appointment. The enthusiastic response from Dr. Enkin and his staff encouraged her to make more.

By the time baby Aaron was born, I had done about eighty cartoons about pregnancy. Murray proudly displayed them, copied them, and gave them to other obstetricians for their ceilings. He kept the originals in a safe place.

Hey, could you get me a sandwich while you're up?...

Don't ever say you can't feel it kicking, Fred.... I waited 2 hours.... then my arm fell asleep...

There's someone in there alright!

Goodness, Mary! Haven't you had that baby yet?!

LIFE ISN'T LIKE THE MOVIES

Part of Dr. Enkin's practice was to ensure pregnant moms were ready physically and mentally to give birth and to care for the baby once it arrived. He was aware Lynn's marriage wasn't terribly solid. Although Lynn was convinced things were fine, she remembers that he strongly suggested she keep an open mind and be aware of how great a responsibility raising a child would be. She never thought parenting was something she might have to shoulder alone.

Baby Aaron arrived on April 11, 1973. He was born into a world of turmoil. Both Doug and Lynn's parents lived on the West Coast, so they didn't really have any support or anyone to help guide them through the murky waters of early parenthood. Lynn tried to find consistent freelance work, while learning to be a mother and maintaining a household on her own. Despite his promise, Doug was drinking heavily and spending many unexplainable nights away from home. Six months after Aaron was born, Doug moved in with a woman he'd been secretly seeing for some time.

I was relieved, actually. In my mind, I had left him many times. To be separated was something for which I was mentally prepared ... or so I thought. I fell apart. I lay on my bed wondering how I could cope. I needed someone who would comfort but not coddle me, someone who would pick me up, set me down, and get me straightened around. I called Marjorie Baskin.

She came to my house immediately, kicked off her boots, lay down on my couch, and said, "You think *you've* got problems! Try living with a rabbi! [Her husband, Rabbi Bernard Baskin, has been a dear friend to me, too.] I can't even go to a coffee shop with one of my male colleagues without somebody calling my husband!" She made me laugh. Then she told me to make a plan for each day — don't focus on the future, just take it day by day. The deal was I wouldn't criticize her and she wouldn't criticize me ... we'd leave criticism to relatives!

This is one of the most autobiographical cartoons from this period — this drawing is essentially a portrait of Lynn's family, 1973.

Elly's friend Annie struggles with the same doubts that kept
Lynn from confronting Doug about his infidelities.

Lynn and Doug were divorced. He took what he could on his motorcycle and left. He told her she could "have the house, the kid, the car, the dog, and everything else, and after that, not to expect him to contribute anything." She was, for the first time, on her own and in complete control of her life. She was empowered by her freedom, but financial independence was another matter.

Lynn and Aaron had become a team
of two after Doug's departure, 1975.

My freelance business was generating about $7,000 a year, and I was thrust [into] a stage of adulthood I have never experienced before — complete independence. [...] With a baby on my back, I peddled my folio from ad agency to ad agency, getting small jobs here and there. I did posters, billboards, television graphics, medical illustrations. [...] It felt good to joke about divorce and being single. It felt good to joke about feeling ugly and inadequate and unloved. It felt good to joke about the burdens of parenthood. I went back to the old family trait of, "If you can't say it right out — joke about it."

It wasn't long before Lynn realized she couldn't survive on freelance wages alone, and she was forced to find full-time work.

Through friends at an advertising agency, she got a job at Standard Engravers, a packaging firm in the industrial part of Hamilton. Here her education as a graphic artist continued. For

Panel 1: ELLY...IF YOU DIDN'T KNOW I HAD LAWRENCE...

Panel 2: WOULD YOU SAY THAT I LOOKED SINGLE?

Panel 3: I'D SAY YOU LOOKED LIKE AN ATTRACTIVE GIRL, PAST HER TWENTIES.

Panel 4: I LOOK DIVORCED AND ON THE MAKE, DON'T I?

Connie often expressed the insecurities Lynn had as a single mother.

the two years she worked there, she learned about typesetting, packaging, printing, photography, and line quality. She learned to use brushes, set squares, French curves, and technical pens on all kinds of different surfaces. Despite enjoying the camaraderie and the challenge of working at Standard Engravers, it wasn't long before she was playing the fool and risking her job.

I finally landed a full-time job in the layout department of a packaging firm. Welfare covered Aaron's daycare costs — I'll be forever grateful for that. I was not the best of employees. I hated being at work by 8:30. I found the endless stream of cereal boxes, fertilizer and medicine packages, and sketches of farm machinery a tiresome chore. I clowned around a lot. If the place (a factory, actually) could not have a colorful décor and cheerful surroundings then, by golly, they had *me*! My supervisor put up with a great deal. I was a comic and a nuisance, but he cared for me enough to keep me on.

(above right) Lynn at a friend's home studio, catching up on what couldn't be done on the job. She often put in unpaid overtime.

(left) A sample product from Standard Engravers: a cereal box featuring a finger puppet cut-out Lynn designed.

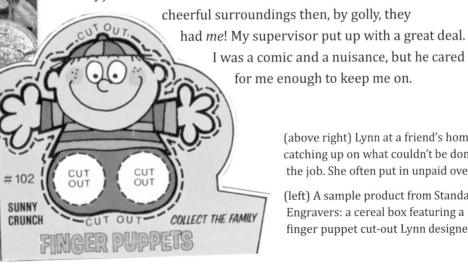

CRUNCHY GRANOLA
honey almond
737 g 26 oz

#102 SUNNY CRUNCH

CUT OUT
CUT OUT

CUT OUT   COLLECT THE FAMILY
FINGER PUPPETS

Privately, Lynn recalls, she was lonely, overworked, and unhappy. Her saving grace was a friendship she had made with a single mother of three, who was also on welfare. Adrienne "Andie" Parton offered the support Lynn needed, and Lynn was there for Andie just the same.

When we needed a friend most, it was often at 3:00 in the morning, when most people are asleep. Andie could call me anytime, and I could call her. We didn't use this safety net often, but when we did, the conversation was always loving and understanding.

It was Andie's idea to go to bed "beautiful." When you're lonely and alone, you look in the mirror after you've been crying and your first thought is, "Who would want me? Look at how ugly I am!" We went to the Salvation Army Store — Andie pushing baby Christopher and

toddler Stephen in a stroller, and I carried little Aaron on my back. We bought the slinkiest and most outrageous nightwear we could find, the kind a new bride might get as a gag gift for her wedding night. We agreed to do our hair and our makeup, put on the gowns, and phone one another before we went to bed.

Andie would call me and say, "Are you gorgeous, babe? Me too! We might be going to bed alone, but we're the best on the planet, right? Aren't we beautiful?!" We didn't feel so lonely; we had each other.

(left) Lynn and Andie, here in the late '90s, have maintained an incredibly close relationship over the years — they are like family.

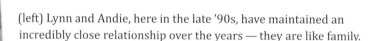

Lynn found endless amusement watching Aaron in his Jolly Jumper,
and she later enjoyed drawing this into the strip.

It was Marjorie's common sense and Andie's upbeat personality that
kept me both sane and stable during a pretty awful time in my life.

Lynn continued to work full-time and freelance on the side — sometimes this meant staying up all night to ensure a client's job would be done on time. Still, with a mortgage to pay, a car to insure, and groceries to buy, she was finding it hard to manage.

I was beginning to hate my full-time job. I had a folio full of illustrations, some done to accompany a poem I had written for Aaron and others that were done on spec. I took my folio to several children's book publishers, hoping to find someone who needed an illustrator. I was always turned down.

On top of Lynn's everyday stress of raising and supporting her son on her own, she also had the big dog to contend with.

One day, when Aaron was in the Jolly Jumper, Farley took a run at him, spinning him around like a top. Aaron was fine, but I could see the dog was jealous, and it wouldn't be long before this resentment would take a serious turn.

Not knowing what to do, Lynn contacted the Old English sheepdog owner's association and asked for advice. They found a new home for Farley-the-dog, and he was soon en route to a farm in the country. It was the best thing for Farley at the time, which made Lynn's decision easier.

83

HMMM..... I'M NOT A BAD SWIMMER FOR SOMEONE OVER 40 !!

IN FACT.... I THINK I'M A BETTER SWIMMER **NOW** THAN I'VE **EVER** BEEN !!

THAT DEFINITELY PROVES ONE THING ...

....CELLULITE FLOATS...

YEAH, WE CAN STRIP THE COLOR OUT AN' PUT IN PURPLE STREAKS.

CAN I MOM?

IT'S YOUR HAIR.

OK, WE HAVE ROSE VENOM, MAD MAGENTA LOUD LILAC AND MAJOR SHOCK.

MAJOR SHOCK! I WANNA GO FOR MAJOR SHOCK!

AAAH!

WHATCHA DOING, MOM?
EMPTYING OUR DRAWERS SO THAT YOU CAN MOVE INTO THIS ROOM
LOOK. I FOUND YOUR GRADE ONE REPORT CARDS, LOCKS OF YOUR HAIR, BABY TEETH - AND MIKE'S CUB SCOUT PIN!
SIGH - THE THINGS YOU FIND AT THE BOTTOM OF YOUR LINGERIE DRAWER!
GIVE ME THAT!!!
LYNN

FOR BETTER OR FOR WORSE
BY LYNN JOHNSTON
the MAG to HAVE
SUBSCRIBE NOW!
BEAUTY TIPS
GUYS
GLAMOURTEEN
CANADIAN GE
BEAUTIFUL BROWS
POINK!!!
OW OW OW
OW
OW
POINK!
OW OW OW
OW
OW
OW OW
OW
SNIFF
OW!
MAYBE I'M TOO YOUNG TO BE BEAUTIFUL.
LYNN

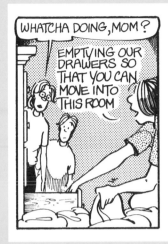

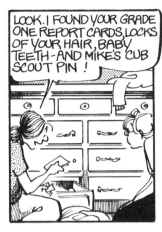

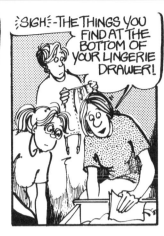

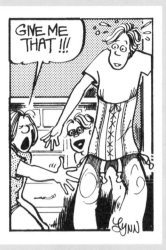

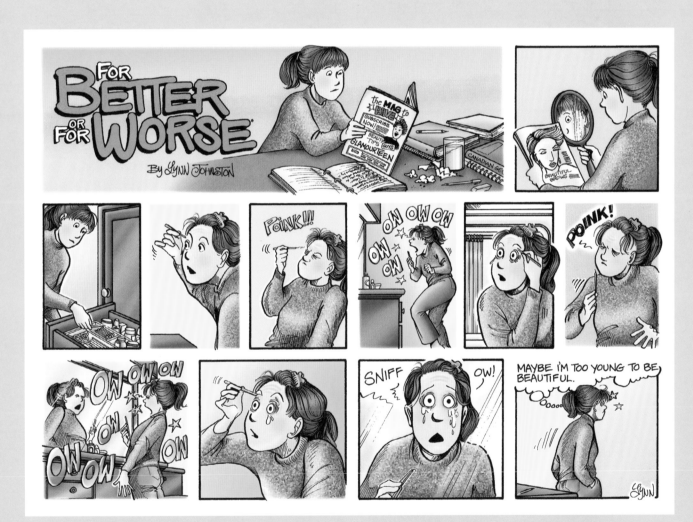

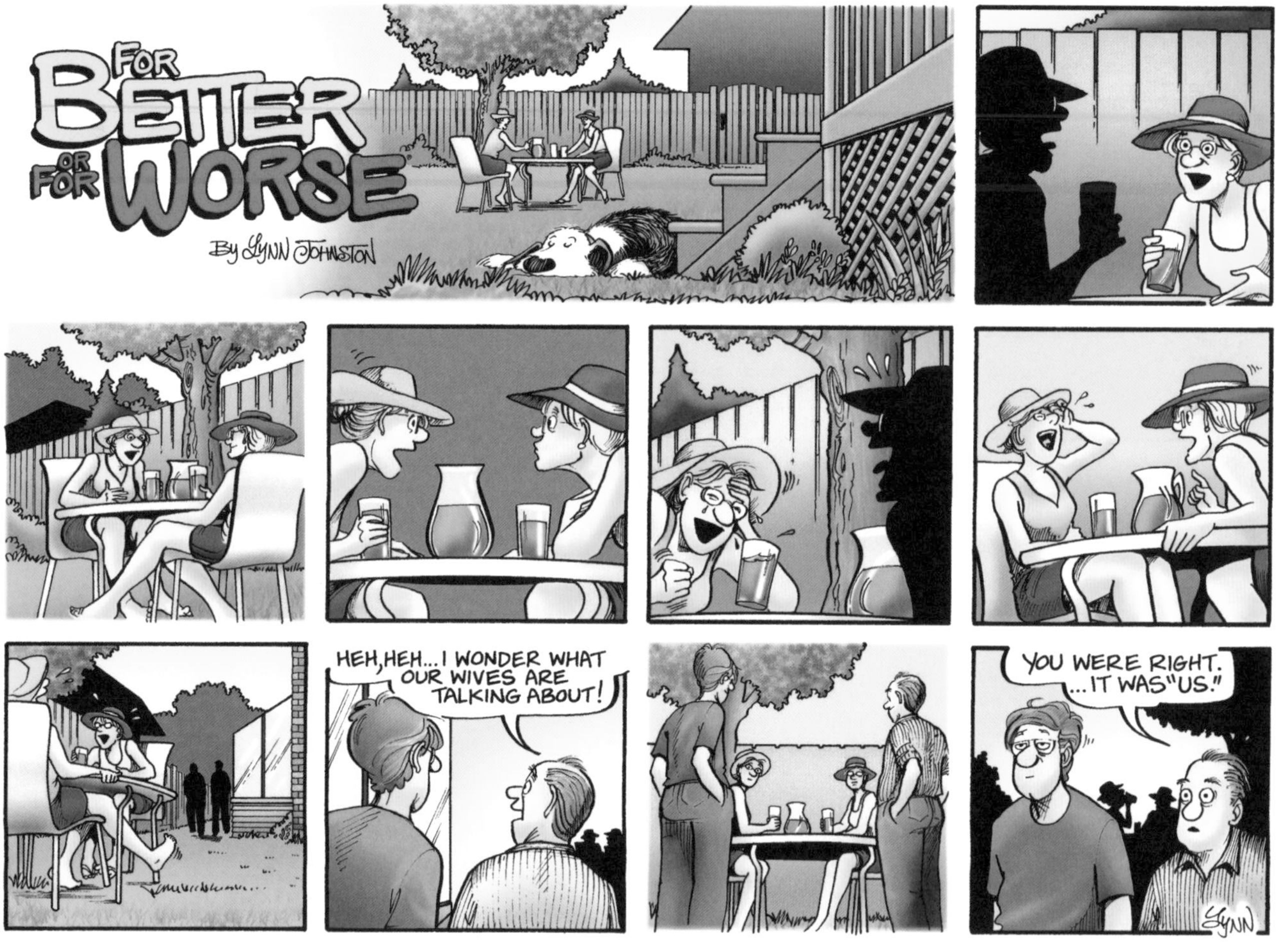
FOR BETTER OR FOR WORSE
BY LYNN JOHNSTON
HEH, HEH... I WONDER WHAT OUR WIVES ARE TALKING ABOUT!
YOU WERE RIGHT. ...IT WAS "US."
LYNN

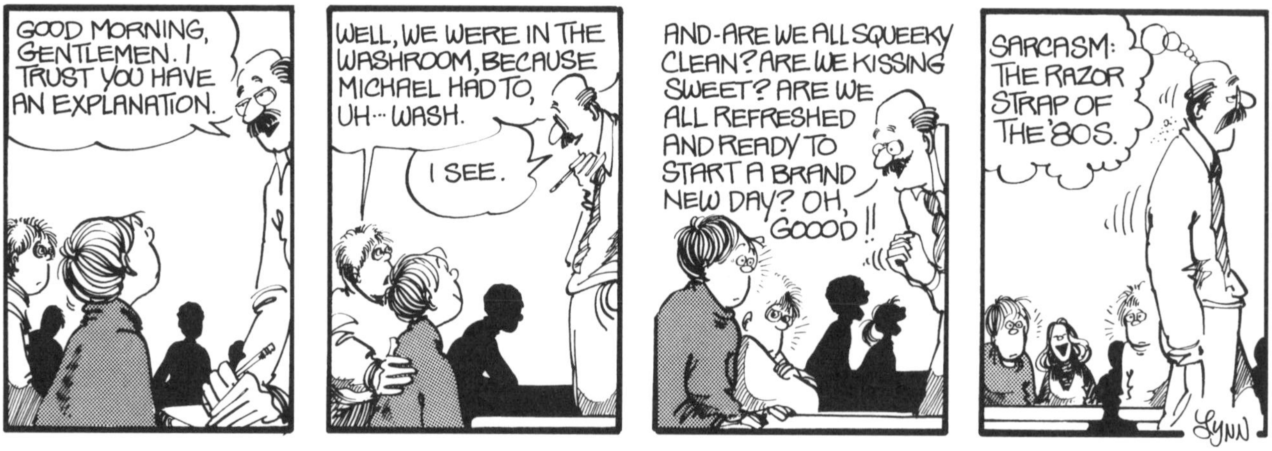
GOOD MORNING, GENTLEMEN. I TRUST YOU HAVE AN EXPLANATION.
WELL, WE WERE IN THE WASHROOM, BECAUSE MICHAEL HAD TO, UH... WASH.
I SEE.
AND-ARE WE ALL SQUEEKY CLEAN? ARE WE KISSING SWEET? ARE WE ALL REFRESHED AND READY TO START A BRAND NEW DAY? OH, GOOOD!!
SARCASM: THE RAZOR STRAP OF THE '80S.
LYNN

OOH-OW-OOOCH-OUCH!! WALK SLOWER, DAWN! THERE'S STONES ON THE SIDEWALK!

HOW COME YOU'RE NOT WEARING SHOES?

I FORGOT.

THEN, I GUESS THERE'S ONLY ONE THING WE CAN DO...

OOH OW! OOH

OOH OUCH! OW!

For Better or For Worse
By Lynn Johnston

IS THIS THE PLACE?

UH HUH.

I'M REALLY SORRY, LIZ.

THANKS. ME TOO.

I'M GLAD THEY LET US BURY HIM HERE. WE'RE GOING TO CALL THIS FARLEY'S TREE. WHEN IT'S WARM ENOUGH.... WE'RE GOING TO PLANT SOME FLOWERS.

NICE.

I DIDN'T THINK I'D MISS HIM LIKE THIS, DAWN. I NEVER THOUGHT THAT A DOG COULD MEAN SO MUCH.

I KNOW.

SOMETIMES, I THINK I'LL SEE HIM AGAIN. I TRY TO IMAGINE WHAT HEAVEN IS LIKE... WHAT IT'S LIKE TO BE THERE.

DO YOU BELIEVE IN GHOSTS, ELIZABETH?

NOT REALLY.

BUT IT'S STRANGE ...AND PROBABLY MY IMAGINATION.

WHAT?

... SOMETIMES, I HEAR THE SOUND OF HIS COLLAR..... AS IF HE WAS WALKING RIGHT HERE.

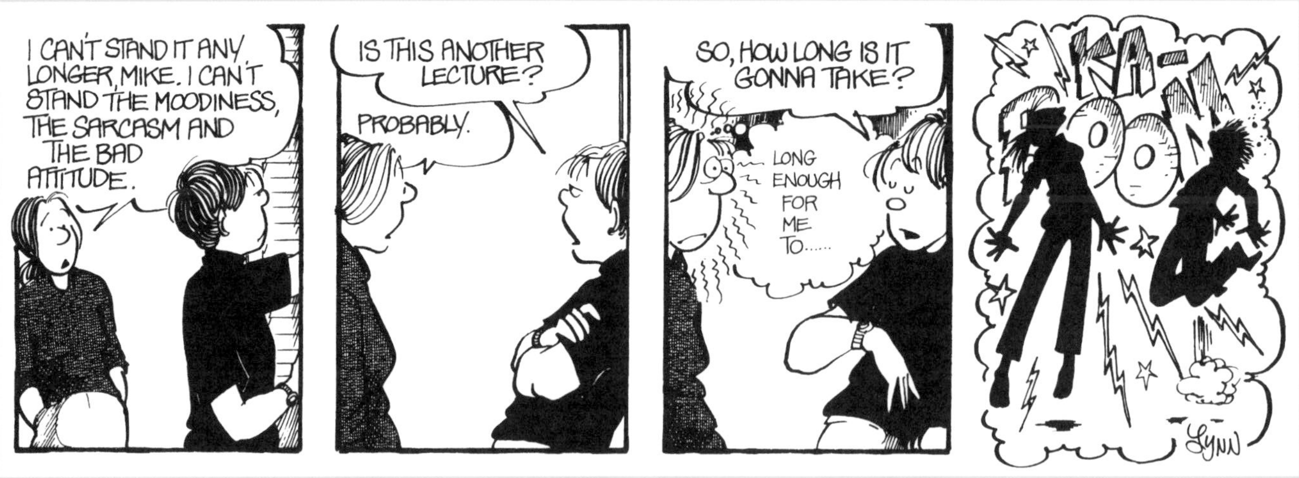
I CAN'T STAND IT ANY LONGER, MIKE. I CAN'T STAND THE MOODINESS, THE SARCASM AND THE BAD ATTITUDE.
IS THIS ANOTHER LECTURE?
PROBABLY.
SO, HOW LONG IS IT GONNA TAKE?
LONG ENOUGH FOR ME TO......
KA-BOOM!
LYNN

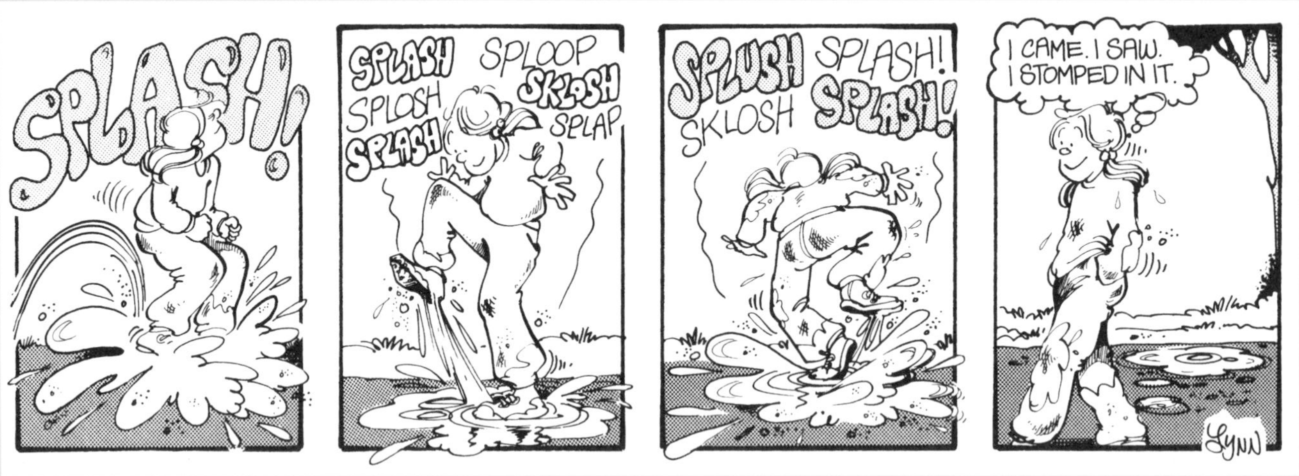
SPLASH!
SPLASH
SPLOOP
SPLOSH
SKLOSH
SPLASH
SPLAP
SPLUSH
SPLASH!
SKLOSH
SPLASH!
I CAME. I SAW. I STOMPED IN IT.
LYNN

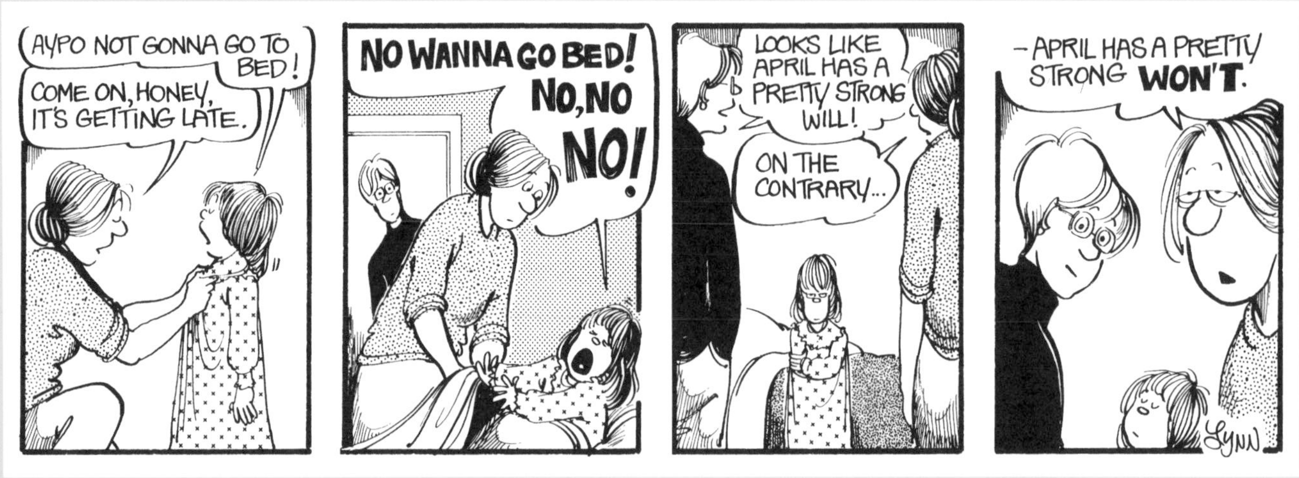
AYPO NOT GONNA GO TO BED!
COME ON, HONEY, IT'S GETTING LATE.
NO WANNA GO BED! NO, NO NO!
LOOKS LIKE APRIL HAS A PRETTY STRONG WILL!
ON THE CONTRARY...
- APRIL HAS A PRETTY STRONG WON'T.
LYNN

Lynn was still in contact with Murray Enkin. One day he called out of the blue to say he had something he wanted to discuss with her and to invite her for dinner. She happily agreed.

> I arrived with kid in tow. His dear wife, Eleanor, opened the door and led us, with a mischievous smile, into the living room. Murray sat on the floor with all eighty cartoons I had drawn for his ceiling, spread around him in order, like a great fan.
>
> "Kid," he said, as he popped the cork out of a champagne bottle, "you've got a book."

Marjorie and Bernard Baskin, friends of the Enkins', had an antiquarian book dealership and knew a lot of people in the business. With their help and Murray's persistence and encouragement, Lynn was able to find a local publisher. Murray became her editor and suggested she increase the number of cartoons to 101. In 1974 Lynn's first book, *David, We're Pregnant!*, was published under the name Lynn Franks.

David We're Pregnant! was not a bestseller, but because it addressed a topic that was somewhat taboo at the time, it garnered a lot of interest.

Lynn's first book, *David, We're Pregnant!*, was later published under the name *Lynn Johnston* with a different publisher.

The only other cartoon book about pregnancy that I knew of was *Eggbert*. It had come out in the '60s, and to my mother's great discomfort, I'd bought one. Eggbert was an unborn baby in a U-shaped bag. He had all kinds of opinions and comments, one of which I remember: Eggbert is looking through the opening of his bag, at the doctor, one supposes, and saying, "Yoo-hoo, I see you!" It was something very suggestive for the day! This cartoon book was revolutionary.... I had in no way copied *Eggbert*; my cartoons were all about the parents, not the babies. I wanted to show different

PAYCHEQUE
↓

reactions, different nationalities, and different situations. There was really nothing else like it on the market at the time.

Lynn had stumbled upon a niche market in the book industry that was showing real signs of growth. When *David, We're Pregnant!* began to generate a few royalty dollars, Lynn left the job at Standard Engravers to focus her attention on her freelance work. Her goal was to have a full-time, home-based commercial art business.

During my time at Standard Engravers, it was clear to me that I could not work for someone else. I had worked for some wonderful people, but for the most part, my relationship with "the boss" had not gone well. I could not comfortably work with, and take orders from, someone I didn't respect. I always did a good job of the projects I was given, but I became juvenile, a prankster, and a comic thorn in everyone's side. As soon as *David, We're Pregnant!* showed some signs of success, I left my job at Standard Engravers. I was a single mom, willing to take the chance that my freelance work and a book a year might sustain my son and myself. A couple of people were sad to see me go, others were relieved and said so!

Lynn managed to build up quite a few regular clients. She was receiving so much work, that she had to hire her friend Dennis Weir to pick up the slack. Lynn had worked with Dennis in the Art Department at McMaster University.

My work with Dennis began very positively. We were both eager to be on our own — away from the confines of the university and independent

from the ad agencies that took our ideas but didn't pay us for them! At the time, if you were asked to submit ideas for an ad campaign, for example, they might keep your sketches for "review," reject them, have their "in-house" artists rework your idea, publish it, and claim they had come up with it themselves. This happened to me several times, and I soon learned to mistrust just about anyone who asked for preliminary sketches!

If Dennis and I had been able to work together continuously, there is no doubt in my mind that we would have owned and operated a thriving, and very competitive, advertising agency. He had amazing art and technical skills. He could write and produce everything from fine illustrations to the fast layouts and roughs needed for client presentations. We were well matched as colleagues. When we eventually went our separate ways, Dennis moved to Nova Scotia, where he began a landscaping company. He died of AIDS three years later.

Starting her own business was exciting and rewarding, but Lynn remembers she couldn't help feeling depressed and lonely: she wanted to be part of a couple again.

As a divorcee, I rode the rollercoaster of relationships. I had just come to the end of another gut[-]wrenching and empty ride, and on this particular day, when the sky was overcast and the baby was whining in the car seat behind me, I drove to the local airport. Oh to be able to climb into one of those beautiful, tiny planes and fly away from everything. The sky brightened. I watched a small blue Cessna touch down and taxi toward me. A rather familiar figure emerged and... it was [Rod Johnston] the fellow I'd met at CHCH.

Connie's dating troubles came directly from Lynn's personal experiences.

John Patterson wasn't a pilot, but he enjoyed building models, much as Rod did.

Lynn learned that with his instrument and float ratings training to complete, Rod regularly commuted to the Hamilton Airport, where he was taking flying lessons. He had given up on a career in television and was now in his second year of dental school in Toronto. Once he graduated, his plan was to go back to northern Manitoba, where he had grown up, and provide a travelling service to First Nations communities in the Arctic. He was going to be a "flying dentist": spending one week a month flying to remote villages to offer free services in exchange for goodwill, experience, and the occasional gift of fish or furs. In order to do this, he would have to buy his own plane one day.

Lynn and Rod hit it off. It wasn't long before the new couple had moved in together, into Lynn's Dundas house. Lynn continued with her freelance business during the day while Aaron was in daycare. Rod commuted daily from Dundas to Toronto to finish dental school, which was especially difficult in the winter.

Christmas was approaching, and Rod had made plans (long before he met Lynn) to visit his brother, who was studying in Scotland. Feeling badly that Lynn and Aaron were going to be alone at Christmas, he suggested she travel to British Columbia to visit her family, and while she was there, she could meet his parents. They were looking after a weaving studio for a few weeks for a friend in Victoria and would love to meet her.

> Aaron and I made the long trek to Victoria. When I knocked on the door, a tall, strapping fellow answered and said, "Ruth, our girl is here!" Then Tom [Rod's father] gave me a great big bear hug and laughed. It was the most amazing welcome from complete strangers. They were nothing like my parents. I remember thinking, "I want this family. I will do whatever it takes to be a part of this family."

There was only one snag. If Lynn wanted to marry and have a future with Rod, she would have to pack up the life she knew in Dundas and move north. Meeting his parents was the deciding factor.

> I agreed to sell my house and go north, but I couldn't imagine living in a tiny Arctic community where I knew nobody and wouldn't be able to continue my work. I asked if we could go to Lynn Lake, where his parents lived. There was a good airport, and he'd be able to travel to many small isolated communities from there. He agreed to the compromise.

(top) Ruth and Tom Johnston, 1980s.

(bottom) William and Carrie Patterson looked very much like Rod's parents, Ruth and Tom.

93

Lynn and Rod were married by Rabbi Baskin in February of 1975. Lynn's mother, though not in attendance, made Lynn's dress, and Marjorie baked the cake. The small ceremony was held in the Baskins' living room. Only the Baskins, Lynn's brother Alan, and a few close friends were there.

It would be a full year before Rod was finished school, and they would be ready to leave Ontario. Although Rod's schooling was covered by student loans, and Lynn continued to eke out a living with her freelance business, money was tight. The summer was approaching, and Rod was on the hunt for summer employment. Rod's sister, Beth, and her husband, Don, offered them work as labourers on their farm. With a family to feed and bills to pay, the offer was hard to pass up. They headed for Manitoba with young Aaron in tow.

We worked from May to September. Rod and Don built a pig barn, put up grain bins, and worked on the tractors out in the fields. I cooked and cleaned and helped Beth in her veterinary clinic. It was such a busy time. There were no children on the farm, and Aaron was in constant danger of getting hurt. […] Rod's mom and dad came down from the north to look after him, and they were wonderful. Those months in Manitoba changed me so much. They introduced a city kid to the life-and-death, matter-of-fact business of running a farm. It wasn't something I instantly took a shine to, either. I went from eager beaver to pain-in-the-arse and back again. I learned to drive a combine, to look up and see a prairie storm coming from miles away, to appreciate where food comes from and how hard it is to grow. There is no one more innovative, patient, or business savvy than a farmer! The farm is where you learn to make things yourself, to rely on each other, and to accept the fact that dirt will enter your house through every portal no matter what you do, so live with it and clean up when it rains.

Lynn soon realized she could live anywhere — as long as she was with family and the people she cared for.

(above right) Lynn and Rod with Aaron on their wedding day, February 15, 1975.

(left) Lynn's drawing of Elly and John on their wedding day.

94

Lynn, after spending several hours helping Beth castrate piglets in her home-based veterinary clinic, 1976.

THE CONTRACT!

Before Lynn met Rod, she had been working on a sequel to *David, We're Pregnant!*, entitled *Hi Mom! Hi Dad!*. She began to have problems with her publisher before the contract for this second cartoon book was signed. Her biggest complaint: he didn't pay her, although *David, We're Pregnant!* was still earning royalties. She had also done illustrations for the same publisher on a series of books called *The Canadian Children's Annual*; payment for this work was withheld, too.

One day, the publisher came to my door and demanded an illustration, which was well overdue for the annual. I refused to give him the art unless he paid me for my book and for other jobs. He said he didn't have the money and asked if there was anything he could do to make me release the art, which he needed that day. I looked at him with disgust and said, "Mow my lawn." He did. It was a very big lawn. I gave him the drawing he needed and vowed to find a new publisher for the second book. That must be the only instance on record where a publisher mowed an author's lawn!

Shortly after this, Lynn met a new publisher from Toronto, who published *Hi Mom! Hi, Dad!*. Even though the book sold well, he didn't pay Lynn either.

When Lynn began work on a third book, she also began to look for a third publisher.

Lynn's second book, *Hi Mom! Hi Dad!*,
was published in 1977, and the cartoons
covered the first year of parenthood.

Lynn's third book, *Do They Ever Grow Up?*,
was published in 1978 and featured
a collection of cartoons about
"the terrible twos and beyond."

An American publisher had seen my books, and by the time I finished
Do They Ever Grow Up?, he was interested in producing all three little
books. He managed to secure the American rights for all three, but the
Canadian rights for *David, We're Pregnant!* remained with the Canadian
publisher — who still hadn't paid me. Much later, I was able to buy
the Canadian rights back from him for the amount that he owed me:
$25,000! As a single mom at the time, I sure could have used that money.

I was now signed with my new American publisher, Meadowbrook
Press. The president and editor of Meadowbrook, Bruce Lansky, made
me take a second look at my drawing — he said it just wasn't good
enough, and it all had to be redone. I was outraged! I thought my work
was fine. I wasn't used to people telling me my work wasn't as good as it
could be.

Once I was able to look more objectively at what I'd done, I had to
admit he was right. I redrew all three books, including the covers. The
new ones were coloured and stood out from the first productions. This
was classy stuff! The three books were beginning to sell as a set, and
ideas for other collections were being discussed.

A selection of cartoons from *Hi Mom! Hi Dad!*

A selection of cartoons from *Do They Ever Grow Up?*

By the summer of 1977, Rod was just finishing dental school, and the family was preparing to move to Lynn Lake. Lynn was now pregnant with Kate. Life was busy (and slightly traumatic) for Lynn, who was about to move away from friends she had made and a place that had become home.

A few weeks before the move, Lynn received a phone call from someone at Universal Press Syndicate (UPS), in Kansas City, Missouri, to ask if Lynn would be interested in applying for a job to create a regular, daily comic strip for syndication.

> My three little books had found their way to the desk of Jim Andrews, who, with the success of Cathy Guisewite's *Cathy*, was looking for a cartoonist to do a strip on family life from a woman's point of view. He wanted something contemporary, a little controversial perhaps. Based on the work they had seen, Jim and his associates thought I might be capable.
>
> We were living out of boxes. Never one to refuse a challenge, I fired off twenty comic strips to Universal Press Syndicate. I had never developed a set of characters. The only people I knew I could draw over and over again were my family, having doodled cartoons of us on the countless letters I wrote home. The twenty strips featured the Johnston family. We waited for a response from the syndicate, never really expecting to hear from them again.

It wasn't long before Lynn was contacted by UPS again. They liked what they saw. Before she knew it, she was on a plane to Kansas.

> Sitting across from Jim Andrews, Lee Salem, and John McMeel at the large rosewood table in their boardroom was terrifying. Despite the enthusiasm and confidence radiating from the faces of these articulate,

well-dressed people, I was a mess of indecision. I knew I could produce a book a year, but could I be funny, or at least worth reading, every single day? A merciless deadline, I couldn't imagine. What boundless inner resources one would have to possess before agreeing to something like this?

Eventually […] they left me alone in the room with the dreaded contract. In the moments that followed, I watched my right hand pick up the pen and draw my signature on the bottom line. Everyone seemed pleased. There were handshakes and congratulations and someone suggested that we all go out for lunch. I respectfully declined. I went back to my hotel room and was ill.

Two examples from the first twenty strips Lynn sent to Universal Press Syndicate in 1977.

Lynn, about to have a baby and be uprooted, had just made a 20-year commitment to write and draw a daily comic strip — 365 days of the year for 20 years!

Before her preliminary work began, Lee Salem, her editor and mentor, suggested she call Cathy Guisewite for some advice — from one woman in the profession to another.

> Cathy was wonderful. She told me that she worked from a script — something like the dialogue in a short play. This sounded like a great way to begin the process. She also told me not to use any real family names, as her title "Cathy" had made for some uncomfortable interviews and reader commentary.

Kate was born December 28, 1977, with the help of Dr. Murray Enkin. Two months later, the family moved to Lynn Lake, Manitoba.

Lynn's illustration for a farewell party invitation, 1978.

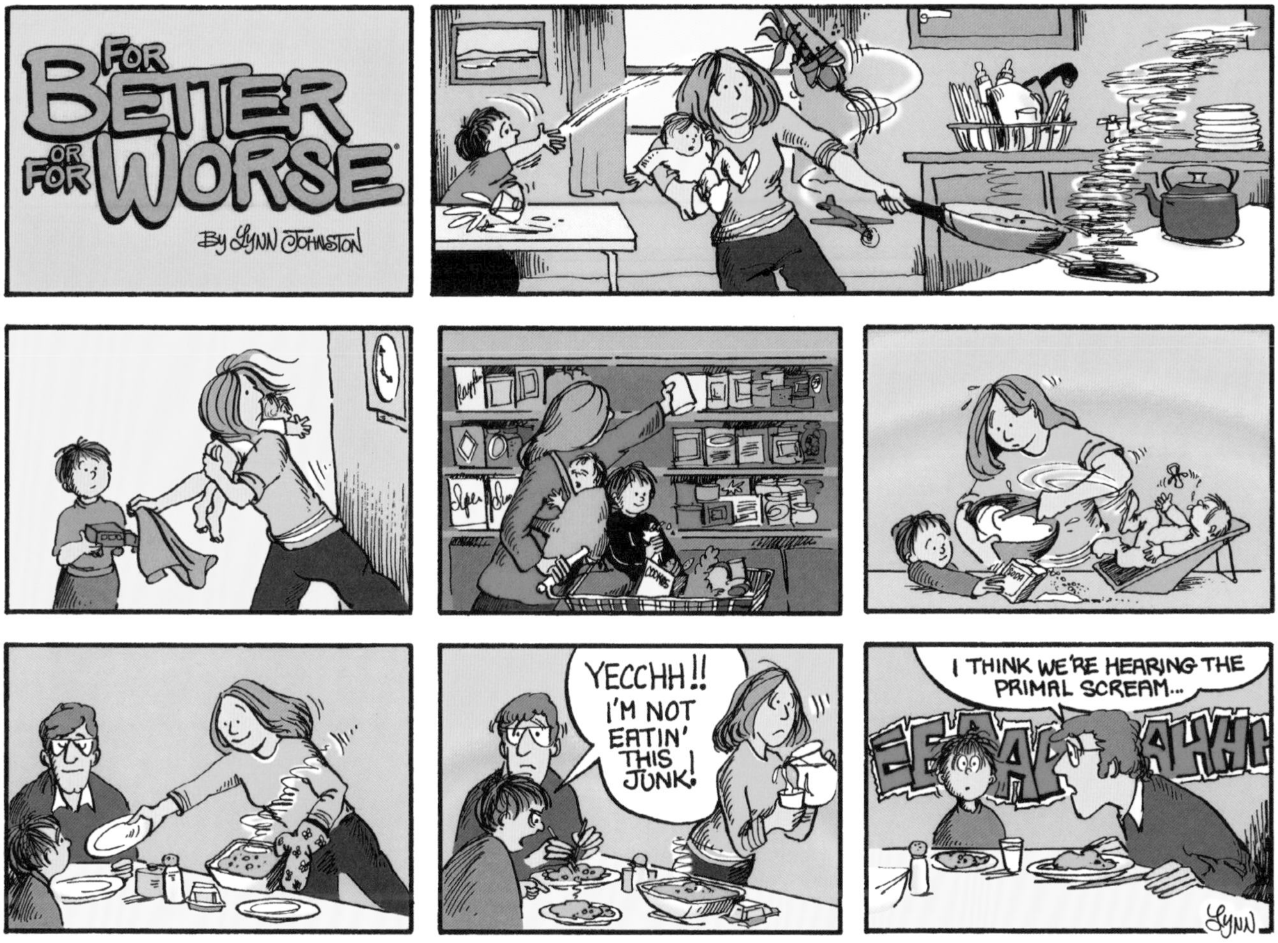
FOR BETTER OR FOR WORSE
BY LYNN JOHNSTON
YECCHH!! I'M NOT EATIN' THIS JUNK!
I THINK WE'RE HEARING THE PRIMAL SCREAM...
EEAA AHHH
LYNN

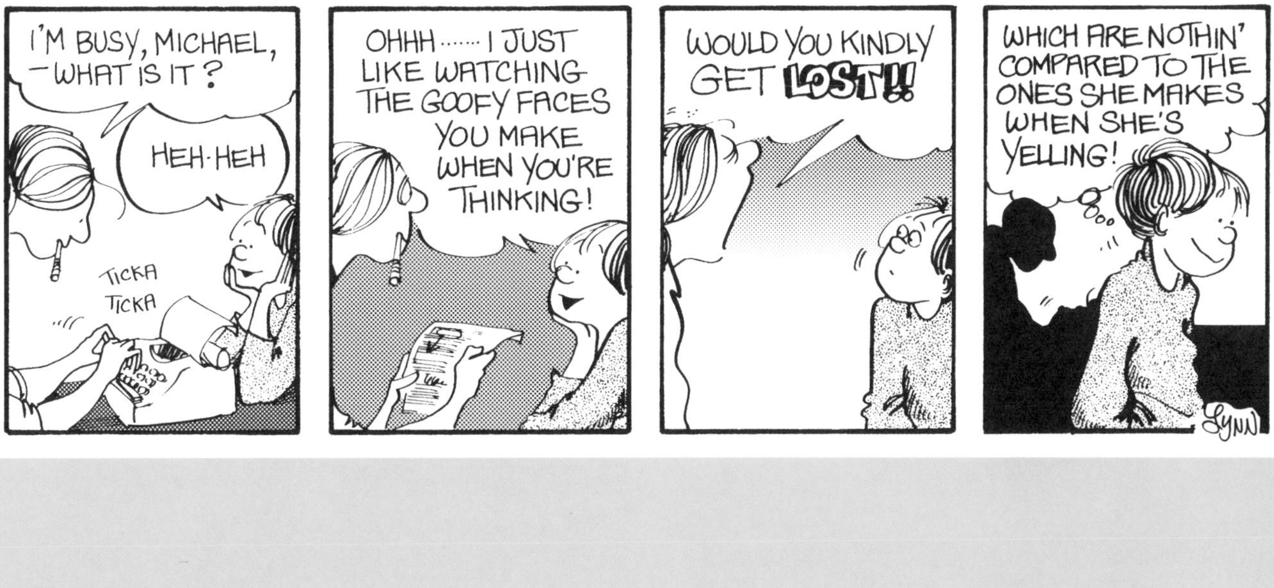
I'M BUSY, MICHAEL, —WHAT IS IT?
HEH·HEH
TICKA TICKA
OHHH....... I JUST LIKE WATCHING THE GOOFY FACES YOU MAKE WHEN YOU'RE THINKING!
WOULD YOU KINDLY GET LOST!!
WHICH ARE NOTHIN' COMPARED TO THE ONES SHE MAKES WHEN SHE'S YELLING!
LYNN

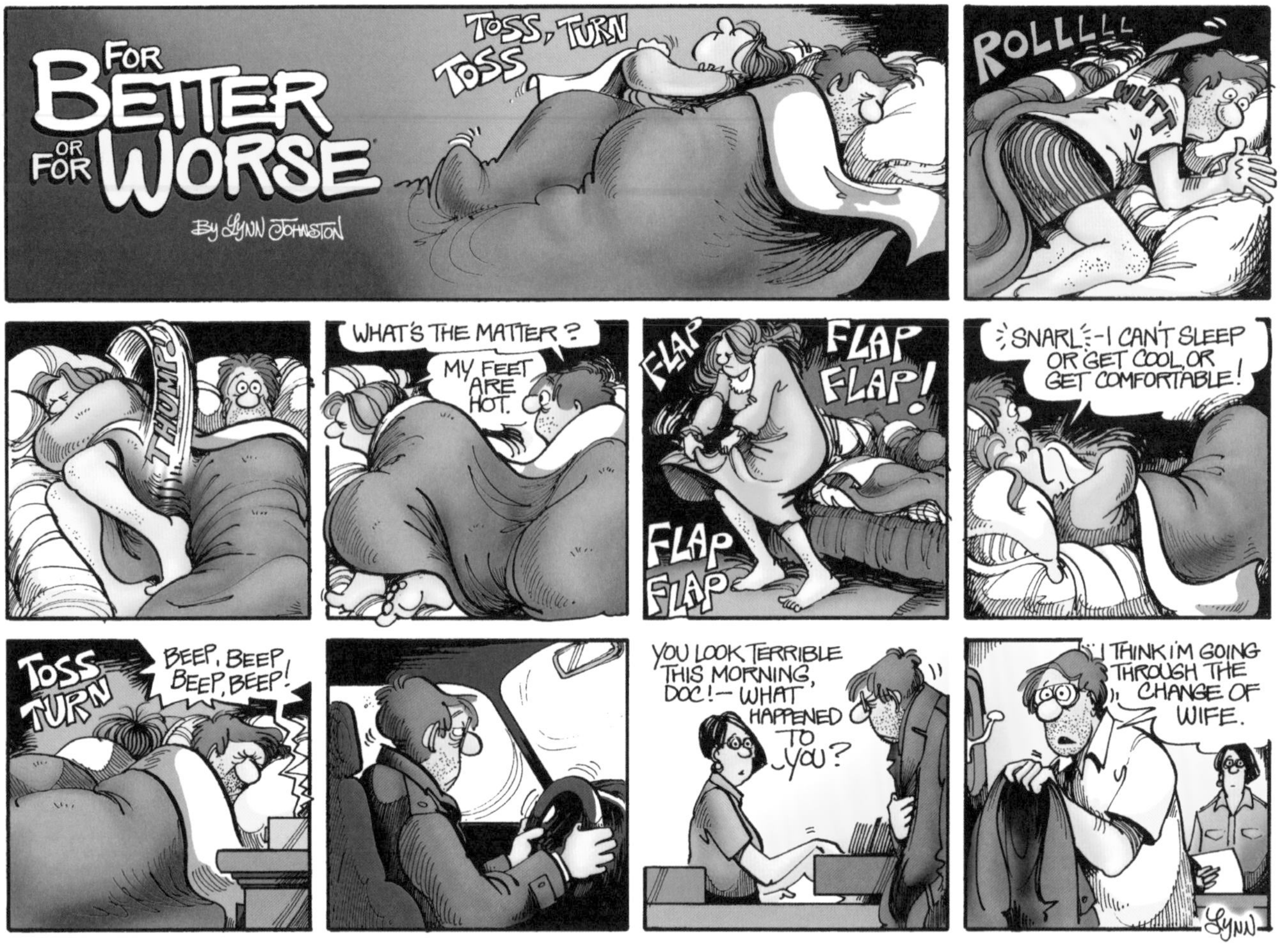
FOR BETTER OR FOR WORSE
BY LYNN JOHNSTON
TOSS, TURN
TOSS
ROLLLLL
WHAT'S THE MATTER?
MY FEET ARE HOT.
FLAP
FLAP
FLAP!
FLAP
FLAP
SNARL -I CAN'T SLEEP OR GET COOL, OR GET COMFORTABLE!
TOSS
TURN
BEEP, BEEP
BEEP, BEEP!
YOU LOOK TERRIBLE THIS MORNING, DOC! - WHAT HAPPENED TO YOU?
I THINK I'M GOING THROUGH THE CHANGE OF WIFE.
LYNN

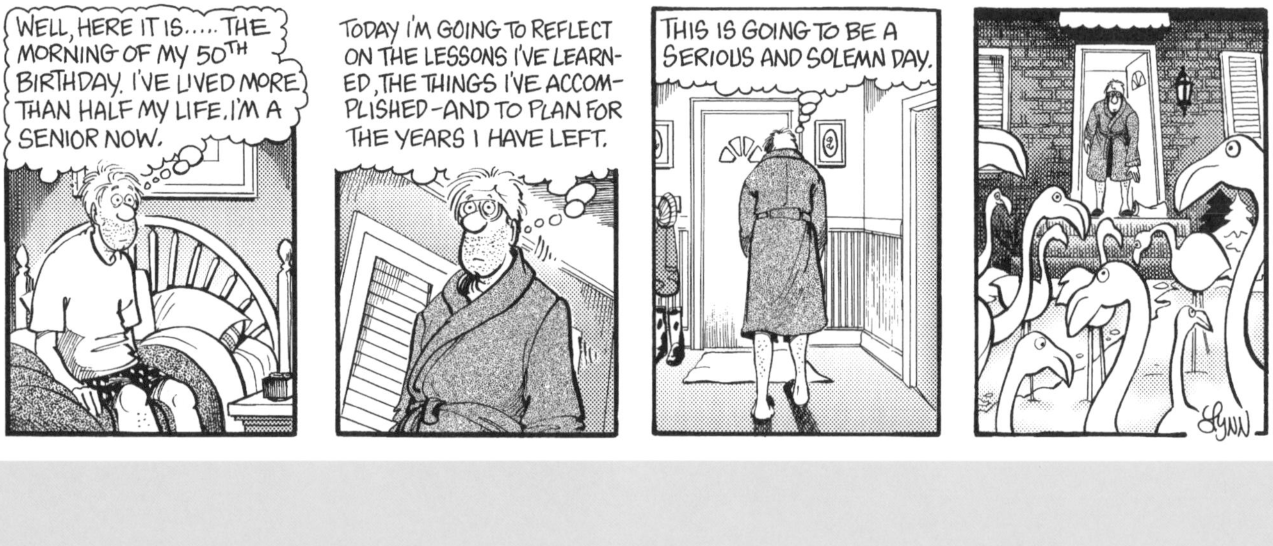
WELL, HERE IT IS..... THE MORNING OF MY 50TH BIRTHDAY. I'VE LIVED MORE THAN HALF MY LIFE. I'M A SENIOR NOW.
TODAY I'M GOING TO REFLECT ON THE LESSONS I'VE LEARNED, THE THINGS I'VE ACCOMPLISHED - AND TO PLAN FOR THE YEARS I HAVE LEFT.
THIS IS GOING TO BE A SERIOUS AND SOLEMN DAY.
LYNN

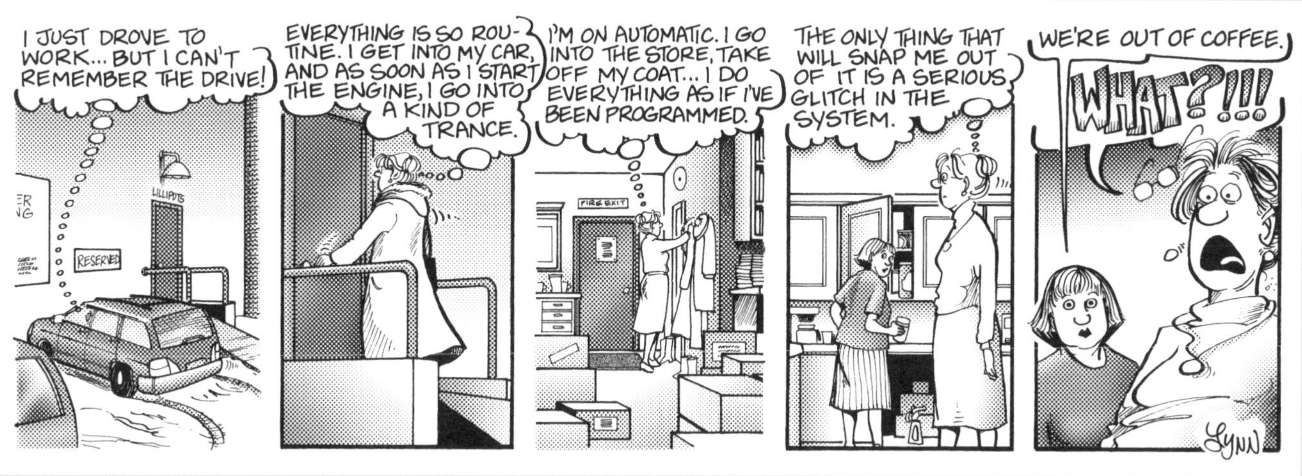
I JUST DROVE TO WORK... BUT I CAN'T REMEMBER THE DRIVE!
EVERYTHING IS SO ROUTINE. I GET INTO MY CAR, AND AS SOON AS I START THE ENGINE, I GO INTO A KIND OF TRANCE.
I'M ON AUTOMATIC. I GO INTO THE STORE, TAKE OFF MY COAT... I DO EVERYTHING AS IF I'VE BEEN PROGRAMMED.
THE ONLY THING THAT WILL SNAP ME OUT OF IT IS A SERIOUS GLITCH IN THE SYSTEM.
WE'RE OUT OF COFFEE.
WHAT?!!!
LYNN

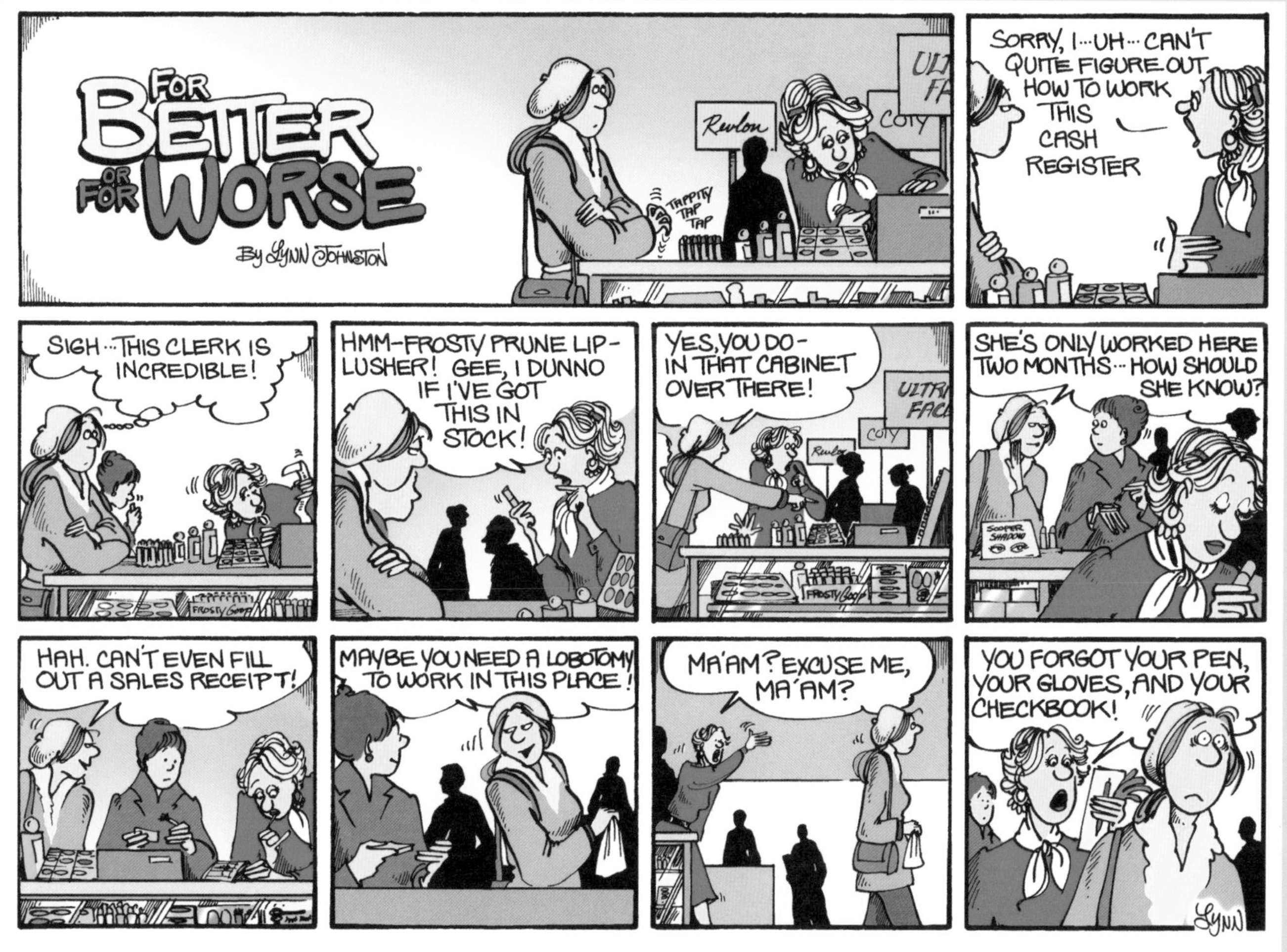
FOR BETTER OR FOR WORSE
BY LYNN JOHNSTON
TAPPITY TAP TAP
Revlon
COTY
SORRY, I...UH...CAN'T QUITE FIGURE OUT HOW TO WORK THIS CASH REGISTER
SIGH...THIS CLERK IS INCREDIBLE!
HMM-FROSTY PRUNE LIP-LUSHER! GEE, I DUNNO IF I'VE GOT THIS IN STOCK!
YES, YOU DO- IN THAT CABINET OVER THERE!
SHE'S ONLY WORKED HERE TWO MONTHS...HOW SHOULD SHE KNOW?
HAH. CAN'T EVEN FILL OUT A SALES RECEIPT!
MAYBE YOU NEED A LOBOTOMY TO WORK IN THIS PLACE!
MA'AM? EXCUSE ME, MA'AM?
YOU FORGOT YOUR PEN, YOUR GLOVES, AND YOUR CHECKBOOK!
LYNN

THE STRIP TAKES SHAPE

Lynn was given six months to move, get settled, and develop her strip before it was to be published. She had signed the contract with UPS without ever before having tried writing or drawing a comic strip.

I had always done my cartoons as single panels. I was going to have to learn how to write dialogue and to sequence the art. Often strips submitted to a syndicate are by artists who have taken years to develop and perfect their characters, their scenarios, and their style. I was brand new at this and scared to death! On the other hand, this was the biggest door that had ever been opened for me! All I could do was my best. I had learned from Marjorie Baskin to always do my best work and to believe in myself. I had learned from Bruce Lansky to take direction when good direction is given and to be smart enough to do something over and over until it is right!

Having based the first twenty strips she had sent to the syndicate on her own family and receiving such rave reviews, it seemed natural to commit to a family-based column. At first Lynn called the strip *The Johnstons*, but she quickly changed her mind after talking with Cathy Guisewite.

With just a short time to go before real daily publication began, Lee Salem asked me to give the family a name. On the spur of the moment, I thought "Patterson" would work: *patter*, as in dialogue, and *son* for the family connection. It was Lee's suggestion that the title of the strip be *For Better or For Worse* because that's what we had decided the strip was going to be about: the ups and downs of marriage and family life. I had been recruited to produce something edgier and closer to the truth, the kinds of things Jim Andrews had seen in my little cartoon books.

Lynn contemplates her new career path from her basement studio on Elgin Drive in Lynn Lake.

Along with the family surname, the first names of the characters had to be altered as well. Lynn decided to change her characters' names to her family's second names: Aaron became Michael, Kate became Elizabeth, and Rod became John. Lynn's middle name is Beverley. She couldn't quite bring herself to use this name for the main character because, "Beverley isn't an easy name to fit into a speech balloon; Bev was too short, and I felt too close to the character anyway to commit to it my own name." Lee was pressuring Lynn to make a decision, as these final details needed to be ironed out as soon as possible.

With only a few days to go before Lynn's finished ink drawings were to be submitted, she decided to name the heroine "Elly" in honour of her childhood friend.

Elly Jansen was my soulmate. I loved her more than I can say. One day we were sitting in the local movie theatre in North Vancouver, and I noticed that she wasn't watching the screen. She had a terrible headache — she was getting them often. Stoic and strong, she sat through the show without complaining. I made jokes to try and cheer her up. Her dad picked us up. Elly was silent as he drove me home. It was Christmastime.

When I returned to school with the rest of the kids in the New Year, Elly wasn't there. Our teacher, Mr. Lowney, called me aside. He asked me to sit down. He told me that Elly had died from a brain tumour and that her funeral would be tomorrow.

I was speechless. I had never been in shock before. I was taken home by one of the custodians. My mother, who was working at the jewellery store, came home to be with me. I sat in my room for the rest of the day and stared at the wall. Worried that I wouldn't be able to handle a funeral, my mother suggested I not attend, but I insisted. I wanted to be there. I had to go.

The funeral home on Lonsdale had an attractive wood-panelled chapel. My mother took my hand and led me to a seat on the aisle — in case we had to leave quickly. Neighbours, teachers, parents, and other students filed in. Elly's family was behind a wall with an opening in it for viewing. I could hear her mother crying, her father soothing her, and her little sister, Lois, asking, "Daddy, where's Elly?"

I had never experienced real grief before. It was unbearable. I cried so hard that my mother tried to put her hand over my mouth, but Mr. Lowney stopped her.

"Let her cry," he said. "Let her cry." When the service was over, everyone began to file past the small wooden coffin where Elly's body lay. My mother tried to lead me away from the coffin, but I pushed forward. I wanted to see her — out of love and curiosity. There were flowers everywhere. The lid of the coffin was lined with satin. Asleep on the pillow was a face I recognized, but it wasn't Elly. It was a lovely young girl with a soft, brown feather headband. Her hands were crossed on her chest. She looked peaceful and somehow wise. I stopped crying. The grief was gone. We left the building through the back door, past the people, past the hearse. Rain was pouring down. I thought rain was appropriate for the kind of day it had been, and I was glad to avoid the cemetery and go home.

Elly wasn't dead. She was gone. If the girl in the coffin wasn't Elly, then she was somewhere wonderful. It wasn't heaven. I refused to think that a kind and loving God would take her away when she had so much to live for. She was only eight years old. I told her then I would love her forever and would remember her for the rest of my life — and I have. Elly's death was a critical event in my life. Few experiences before or since have rocked my world like the death of my best friend. I named the lead character in *For Better or For Worse* after Elly Jansen — it gave me closure, and I think she would be pleased.

Although Elly Patterson was named after Elly Jansen, her personality was certainly based on Lynn's.

As a single mother who ran a potentially successful advertising business, I'd earned a few stripes, so Elly Patterson was destined to reflect my points of view! She was a mirror of me. If she seemed unfulfilled and antagonistic sometimes, I was, too — but aren't we all? Aren't we all unsatisfied, unhinged, uncomfortable, and unhappy once in a while? This is what makes comedy the healing art that it is!

This was the first *For Better or For Worse* comic strip to be published.
The song, "Wives and Lovers" by Burt Bacharach and Hal David, triggered anger
in Lynn (and probably lots of other housewives of the day, too).

When Lynn began drawing *For Better or For Worse*, Elly's character allowed her to express the frustrations of being a homemaker in the 1970s and '80s. The housewife's perspective, underrepresented in mass media at the time, was something women all over North America could relate to. Elly Patterson said out loud what many people were thinking — men and women alike. Today, Lynn finds her early subject matter a bit too negative, but thirty years ago, when she touched on the tedium of being at home with toddlers, guilt at wanting a career, and the sexism many women faced, she was giving vent to issues that women had previously felt they couldn't express publicly. Her approach certainly contributed to the strip's early popularity. Lynn has frequently received the same feedback from many fans, with claims such as, "It's like you're watching from inside my house!"

The other Patterson characters, although loosely based on their namesakes, really represented different parts of Lynn's own personality: "I write and draw myself and my family, but the insights and personal glimpses are, for the most part, scenes from my childhood."

(this page and facing page) Published in 1979, these are the first week of *For Better or For Worse* daily strips. The earliest strips focused on Elly's life as a stay-at-home mom with young kids — and a somewhat clueless and insensitive husband.

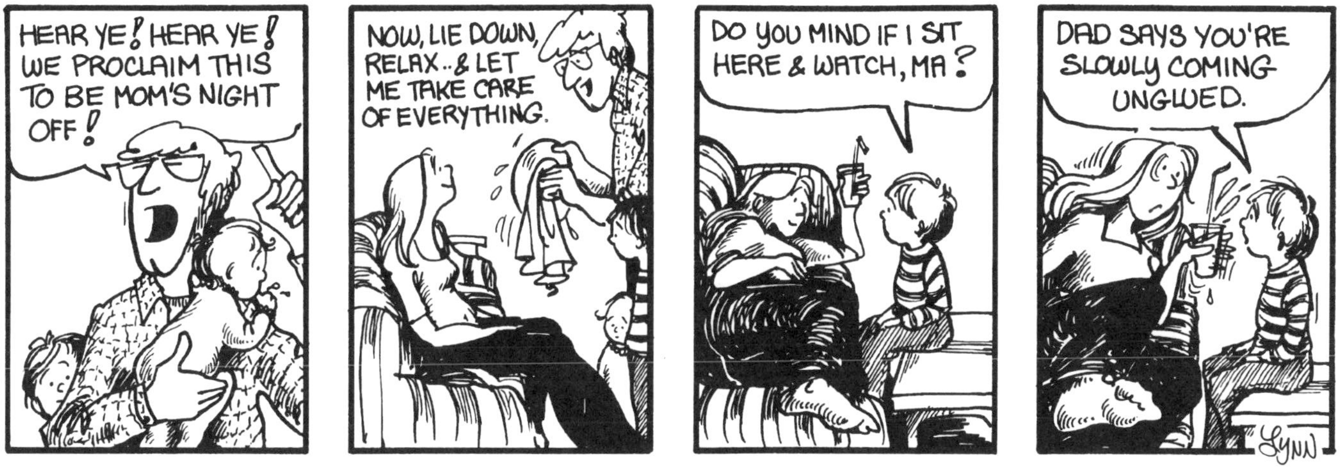
HEAR YE! HEAR YE! WE PROCLAIM THIS TO BE MOM'S NIGHT OFF!
NOW, LIE DOWN, RELAX..& LET ME TAKE CARE OF EVERYTHING.
DO YOU MIND IF I SIT HERE & WATCH, MA?
DAD SAYS YOU'RE SLOWLY COMING UNGLUED.
LYNN

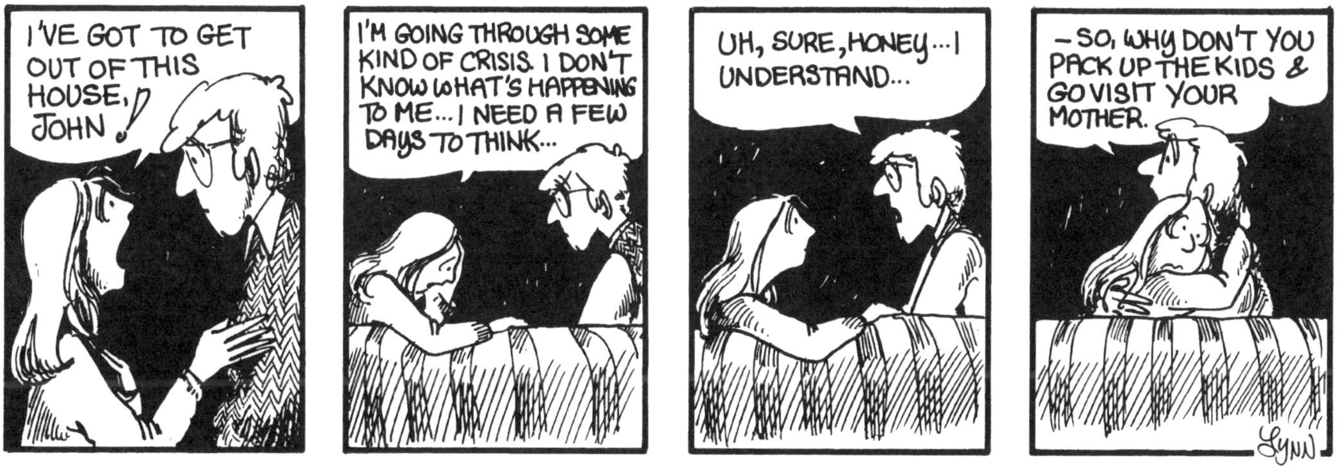
I'VE GOT TO GET OUT OF THIS HOUSE, JOHN!
I'M GOING THROUGH SOME KIND OF CRISIS. I DON'T KNOW WHAT'S HAPPENING TO ME... I NEED A FEW DAYS TO THINK...
UH, SURE, HONEY... I UNDERSTAND...
– SO, WHY DON'T YOU PACK UP THE KIDS & GO VISIT YOUR MOTHER.
LYNN

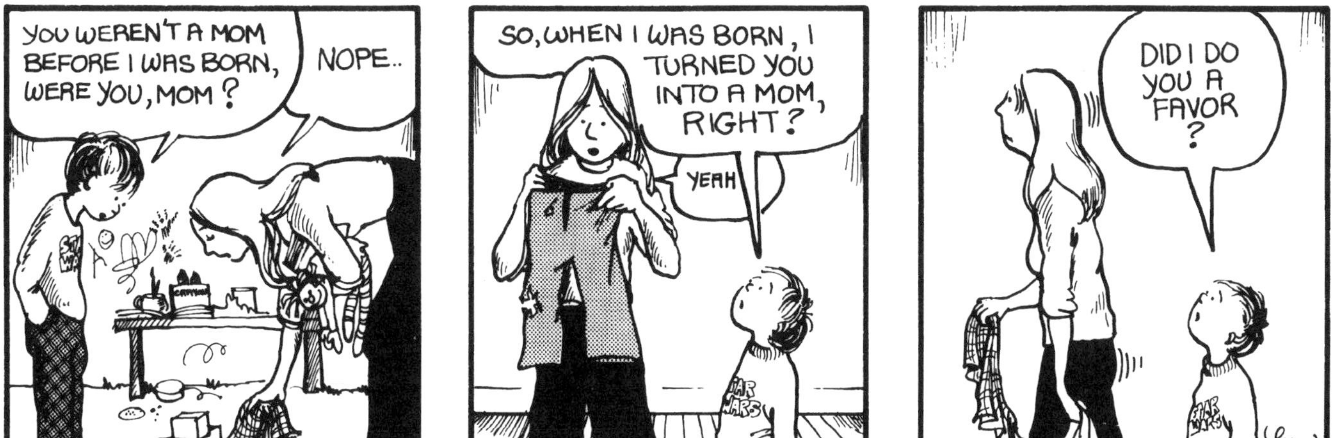
YOU WEREN'T A MOM BEFORE I WAS BORN, WERE YOU, MOM?
NOPE..
SO, WHEN I WAS BORN, I TURNED YOU INTO A MOM, RIGHT?
YEAH
DID I DO YOU A FAVOR?
LYNN

Lee Salem worked directly with Lynn on her ideas and pencil roughs until she felt she was ready to launch. Lynn acknowledges that Lee has been a tremendous resource and mentor for her throughout her entire career.

> Smart, funny, hard-working, and serious about business, Lee became one of Universal Press's most outstanding staff members. Fair and firm, he had a good relationship with all of us cartoonists. He was an excellent editor and drove a hard bargain when it came to disputes and contract negotiations. I was always appreciative of his skilful management and his heartfelt diplomacy. My respect for Lee was another reason to work hard for this job. I have much to thank him for.

Before Lynn knew it, her six months were up, and it was time to start the demanding schedule of writing, drawing, and submitting a daily column six weeks ahead of the publication date — 365 days a year.

When the strip debuted in September 1979, I thought I was ready. The regular faxes to Lee [...] had set me up with a routine, a style, and a few weeks "in the bank," which was a safety net before the crush of the real deadlines began. Strangely enough, I had no problem digging material out of the normal day-to-day stuff that went on around us. The [dental] practice and parenthood provided an endless wellspring of grumbling, which became gags. I was really good at grumbling! The strip was like a sounding board, someone I could talk to about how I really felt.

(above) Lynn used the strip to vent her frustrations, but it also contained many moments of tenderness.

(right) Lynn proud to see her work in print, 1981. Note the comic on the desk is the strip shown above.

LIFE IN A NORTHERN TOWN

For six years, we lived in the small isolated mining town of Lynn Lake, Manitoba. Rod was the local "flying dentist." I produced my strips for Universal Press, took care of the kids, and, from time to time, went crazy. The nearest town was sixty miles away. My friend Nancy and I would sometimes drive there and back — just for donuts! Because there were no shops to speak of, no good restaurants, and no theatre, we new Northerners became an inventive lot. We made our own entertainment, we created our own events, we transplanted city slickers survived, and some of us even grew to enjoy the rustic, laid-back ambience of "the bush."

Gossip was a favourite pastime in Lynn Lake.

(above) The Johnstons' house on Elgin Drive, Lynn Lake, Manitoba, early '80s.

(left) The Johnston family in the living room of their Elgin Drive home, 1979. The couch they are seated on appeared time and again in *For Better or For Worse*.

Lynn worked from a small studio office in the basement of her split-level home. It was bright and quiet and had everything she needed to do the job — a desk and her drawing materials. The most difficult aspect of producing the strip was finding the time to do it. Aaron was thankfully in school by now, and Kate spent the mornings with a babysitter across the street. Lynn worked from nine until noon, and then again after the kids were in bed. The rest of the time she was busy being a mom and maintaining the household. With demanding deadlines to keep on top of and young kids running around, Rod's parents were a boon; they would take the kids day or night, no questions asked.

Ruth and Tom looked after the kids and helped with the strip. They were there for me when my own parents became distant beyond miles. They read every strip and were my best editors. If Ruth didn't get a gag, I knew that a huge per cent of the readers wouldn't get it either, and I'd have to change it. Changing anything was hard — both because my ego would be bruised, and because I had a deadline to hit; any changes took time. Still, real "audience reaction" soon proved to be the best tool in my kit for making my work connect with readers. I never took my strips beyond pencil form before Rod and his parents had read them all and approved them.

Whenever Ruth thought Lynn was getting too much satisfaction from the publicity she was receiving, she would help to put things into perspective. Ruth and Tom kept Lynn's ego in check, as did living in a small, isolated town.

I was, after all, just another mom who took the garbage out like everyone else. In fact, that's why Lynn Lake was the best place I could possibly have been during the early days of the strip; it was far enough away from the city to keep me from accepting interviews, speaking engagements, and empty invitations, which took my time and affected my personality. I found out the hard way that any kind of celebrity, even a small amount, could be dangerous.

By the third year of publication, Lynn's strip had been picked up by over one hundred newspapers and had begun to receive international attention. As the spotlight on Lynn intensified, her time away from her family increased. Her remote location that had buffered her from celebrity early on did not pose an obstacle.

At first, I was excited by the publicity. I felt important. I enjoyed book tours and interviews. I wanted to learn how to do public speaking, so I often accepted opportunities to do so, meaning another trip away from home. I did these engagements for free, wanting to perfect my presentation. I talked while drawing my characters and other goofy things on acetate sheets (the images were projected onto a screen behind me). This is what's called a "chalk talk" in the comic art world, and I managed to get pretty good at it.

Aside from the presentations, eventually Lynn was often required to travel to promote her books. Once a year, a selection of strips from the previous year was packaged into a book and sold across Canada and in the United States. Each fall, Lynn would travel from city to city, store to store, signing books and speaking to the public. These promotional tours offered Lynn opportunities to connect with her growing number of fans, build relationships with Lee Salem and other key people at UPS, and provide an excuse to get out of Lynn Lake for a while.

Despite the small population and relative isolation of her home community, Lynn did her best to fit in to "a town of colorful relationships. It was a town where 'you can steal a man's wife, but you don't touch his woodpile!'" She did what regular parents do: attended school events, parent-teacher interviews, hockey games, and ice skating shows.

(top) Lynn's husband, along with his parents, picked up the parenting slack while Lynn travelled. John's character was somewhat less evolved than Elly's.

(bottom) Lynn holds one of her sketches used for a speaking engagement, early '80s.

CLAUDE AND THE WOODPILE

OH, SING-YE A SAGA OF OL' CLAUDE CHEPIL
THE FOLKS IN THE LEGION, THEY ALL KNOW HIM WELL.
THE MINERS, THE TRAPPERS, THE COPS AN' THE CREE
COULD TELL YOU A STORY ABOUT MR. C!

'TWAS COLD, AN' THE WIND WHISTLED OVER THE TREES,
THE SOUND OF WOOD BEIN' CHOPPED FILLED THE BREEZE,
AS CLAUDE, HIS AXE HONED SO TO SPLIT THE LAST
                                    SPLINTER
HAD MADE HIM A WOODPILE TO LAST THE WHOLE WINTER.

THE LONG NIGHT DESCENDED, THE WOLF AN' THE OWL
STIRRED AS THEY LISTENED TO FOOTSTEPS A-PROWL
AND, PIECE AFTER PIECE OF THAT WOODPILE WAS TOOK
BY SOME HELLUVADAMNSONABITCHUVA CROOK!!

MORNING, SHE BROKE WITH THE USUAL DAWN
AN IT WERE'NT LONG AFORE CLAUDE SEEN HIS WOODPILE
                                    WERE GONE!
"I'LL CATCH ME THAT VARMINT!" HE CRIED O'ER HIS GRUEL
AN' HE SET OFF TO FIND WHAT BECOME OF HIS FUEL.

HE SEARCHED EVERY ALLEY, HE SCOURED EVERY YARD
IDENTIFICATION, HE KNEW, WOULD BE HARD
AT LAST, CHEPIL COME ACCROSS FAST'S AN' THER PILES
HE CLIMBED O'ER THER FENCE, SAID° ID KNOW IT FER
                                    MILES!

YOU TOOK ALL MY WOOD, AN' BY LORDY, YOU'LL PAY!"
GEORGE OFFERED A BEER AN' THAT KEPT HIM AT BAY
WHEN CLAUDE WAS SEDATED, AN' BACK TO HIS SELF,
THEY CALLED THE POLICE, AN' THEY SUMMONED THER
                                    HELP.....

The story of the woodpile theft is true, and Lynn wrote
this poem for her friend's, the victim's, fiftieth birthday party.

"THAR'S A THIEF THAT'S AMONGST US, RIGHT HERE
IN OUR TOWN!
SO, GET OFFA YER DUFFS, AN' GO TRACK THE MAN DOWN!"
IT WERE WELL NIGH TO TUESDAY WHEN THE CULPRIT
WERE FOUND
ALL THEY DID WAS PLUG INTA THE GOSSIP 'ROUND TOWN.
THE NAME THEY COME UP WITH, WERE "NIFTY" THEY SAID.
—"GIVE UP MY DAMN WOODPILE!" SAID CLAUDE
—"OR, YER DEAD!"

NOW, NIFTY, WEREN'T UP TO RETURNIN' NO WOOD.
HE FIGGERED THE WOODPILE WERE HIS, WELL AN' GOOD.

WELL, CLAUDE HE GOT ANGRY. HE SWORE, AN' HE SPIT!
AN' NIFTY BROUGHT BACK A PIECE TOO HARD TA SPLIT.

"FINE! KEEP IT!" CLAUDE COUNTERED, BUT, DON'T CALL
YERSELF WINNER,
FER ONE O' THEM LOG'S GOT A BLASTIN' CAP INNER!"

"YER PULLIN' MY LEG" SAID OL' NIFT WITH A SHOUT.
"JUST BURN 'EM, CLAUDE ANSWERED, "AN THEN WE'LL
FIND OUT!"
—"FOR ONE OF THEM PIECES WILL BLOW YOU TO HELL
SO GO LIGHT UP YER WOODSTOVE, AN' STOKE 'ER UP
WELL."

NOW, NOBODY'S SAYIN' JUST WHAT CHEPIL DONE,
BUT BEFORE HE COULD BURN 'EM, OL' NIFT CHECKED
EACH ONE.
HE INSPECTED EACH PINE CHIP, EACH SPRUCE LOG; HE
PEERED,
AN' EACH TIME HE STOKED UP HIS WOODSTOVE, HE
FEARED
THAT, PERHAPS IT WERE TRUE! MAYBE CLAUDE HAD
RETURNED ......

AND, HAD HIDDEN A CAP IN THE WOOD THAT HE BURNED!

NOW, THAT WOODPILE HAS LONG SINCE BEEN RENDERED
TO ASH

AN' CLAUDE SAYS ELECTRIC HEAT'S WELL WORTH THE
CASH....

BUT, ON COLD WINTER NIGHTS, WHEN THE NORTHERN
LIGHTS GLOWS

CLAUDE SITS AN' REMEMBERS - AN' DEEP DOWN, HE
KNOWS....

IF HE LIVES TO A HUNDERD, AN' LORD KNOWS, HE MAY,
HE'LL SEE THAT OL' NIFTY WILL WELL RUE THE DAY,
HE STOLE CHEPIL'S WOODPILE WITH NARY A CARE —
AN' THE DANGEROUS PART IS, OL' CLAUDE IS HALF
THERE!!

FOR, OUR HERO'S TURNED 50, HIS HAIR'S STREAKED
WITH GREY,

AN' IF ANYTHING ON HIM DON'T WORK, HE WON'T SAY.

SO, LIFT UP YER CUPS, DRINK A TOAST TO CHEPIL!
THE MAN OF THE HOUR'S NOT OVER THE HILL...
HE'S UP ON THE TOP OF IT, READY TO ROAR —
HE'S GOT 'ER IN GEAR, AN' HIS FOOT'S TO THE FLOOR!

AN' HE KNOWS THAT THERE'S LUMPS IN THE ROAD
AFTER 50

AN' HOPEFULLY... ONE OF THEM LUMPS WILL BE
NIFTY.

Happy Birthday, Claude! — from
Rod & Lynn & all the
Johnstons !!

Lynn was a "hockey mom" and did all the work that came with the title. "Klotz" was the last name of a family friend and neighbour in Lynn Lake — Mr. Klotz ran the local auto repair shop.

I was a good mom. If I hadn't been a typical mom, I would never have been able to write from a mom's point of view. Being hands-on was the stuff that went into the Pattersons' everyday lives.

Lynn was able to find just about everything she needed in Lynn Lake. If she needed drawing materials for the strip, the local general store was able to order whatever she requested. If it was a friend she needed, there was always someone within a few minutes' walk from her home. (Indeed, Lynn maintains some of these friendships to this day.) If it was inspiration she was after, Lynn Lake was full of unusual characters, each with a story to tell.

The tiny community of Lynn Lake provided great living resources when I needed auxiliary characters. The philandering, chauvinistic Ted was a composite of two men I knew, and Elly's neighbour, Annie, became more and more like my friend Nancy, with whom I shared both the outpost blues and the challenge of raising two small kids who were indoors much of the time, due to the harsh winters we endured.

Lynn couldn't resist lampooning the locals.

Ted needled John about his life choices and nettled Elly with his outdated attitudes.

Annie and Elly could relate to each other as stay-at-home moms and discussed their lives over coffee.

When Connie decided to move, Elly's despair was familiar to Lynn.

By the mid-1980s Lynn Lake's economy was strained. Tensions mounted as people left the dying town. Kids ran about at night, pushing down fences and breaking windows. Ruth, a retired teacher, and Tom, who was the mill superintendent for Sherritt Gordon, had lived and worked in Lynn Lake for thirty years. Even they were feeling the rejection. The added stress gave the family incentive to move sooner than they had planned.

> It was 1984, and we were mentally separating ourselves from northern Manitoba. Our plan was to stay in Lynn Lake until the population decreased and facilities were closed. We knew this would take some time.

The town became divided between those who were planning to leave and those who would never leave. There was a sense of betrayal as families packed up and moved away. The news that Dr. Johnston and his family would soon be moving, too, did not go over well. After all, Lynn recalls, "we would be taking away the only dental clinic for hundreds of miles. Patients would have to drive to Leaf Rapids, Thompson, or Winnipeg for dental work once we had left."

Lynn Lake had seen much better days. People were finding work elsewhere, shops were closing, windows were being boarded up, and it was time to move on. Many people were setting their sights on Winnipeg, but we liked the north. We wanted to find a place that had the same small-town feel as Lynn Lake and yet had a thriving population.

An illustrated map features the distance from one isolated town to another.

Panel 1: SEE? WHAT DID I TELL YOU! THIS AREA IS STILL WILDERNESS.

Panel 2: UNTOUCHED, UNCHANGED, UNSPOILED BY THE HAND OF MAN...

Panel 4: AMAZING. SOME MOOSE HAS BEEN DRINKING "OLD VIENNA."

A MOVE TOWARDS CIVILIZATION

Lynn and Rod were certain they were going to leave Lynn Lake. They contemplated their options: "We considered moving to BC, but a serious rift between my mother and myself made moving west out of the question." Not interested in moving to Winnipeg, where many Lynn Lake residents were headed, they set their sights on Ontario.

Rod's work required him to do a lot of flying. The aircraft he had purchased when they first moved to Manitoba had been a good plane, but it was getting old. It was evident he would need to get a new one before long. One of the friends Rod had made through the countless hours he had spent at the Lynn Lake airport was a water bomber pilot, Bob Graham, whose parents were living just outside of North Bay, Ontario. Bob suggested this might be a perfect location for Lynn and Rod to relocate: it is considered a northern community, but it is driving distance to both Ottawa and Toronto; it is surrounded by lakes and wilderness; and it had a relatively large population, multiple industries, and a large airport.

> We decided to look at a Cessna that was for sale in Collingwood, Ontario, and went down with the whole family to take a look. It was a good little aircraft. Before making the purchase, we took it for a test flight. We decided to fly up to North Bay. We were advised to fly over Trout Lake and have a look at the scenery.
>
> "But be careful," Bob warned us, "there's a crazy lady on a peninsula who shoots at small aircraft!" Intrigued, we decided to check it out. Figuring that a rifle couldn't reach us at four thousand feet, we circled the property. It was lovely, and it was for sale!

THE NEW HOUSE IN CORBEIL

(above centre) Lynn used her illustration of the back of their log house as her family Christmas card in 1985, shortly after they settled in.

(right) The front of the log house as it appeared from the driveway, 1990s.

A red brick farmhouse was situated on a large field with a number of acres of wooded land behind it. The lake was just steps away. Things began to fall into place. In 1985 Lynn and Rod bought the house, the property, and the airplane too. A few months later, Ruth and Tom moved into the farmhouse — a gift from Lynn and Rod, thanks to the success of the strip. Lynn, Rod, Aaron, and Kate moved into a log house down the road, which had conveniently come up for sale a short time after Ruth and Tom had moved. Once again, they were an easy walk down the road from Rod's parents.

> We were finally living in stable and comfortable surroundings. North Bay is a lovely, old-fashioned community. It has a charming downtown with lots of nice shops, a good airport, multiple grocery stores, couriers, events and activities, and a stable economy. It was a wonderful change. If I couldn't move back to my beloved British Columbia, then I could put roots down here.

Through the kids' schools and the connection to the dental community, they quickly felt welcomed and at home in their new surroundings. They had moved to town at the same time as several other young dental families. (Lynn enjoyed being in a place where her husband wasn't the only dentist.) Instant friendships were made.

> My connection to other dental wives was strong and fast. While our children were school aged, we regularly got together at sporting events, plays, and parties. We shared daily trivia as well as some deep personal truths. These wonderful ladies became the voices behind Elly's close friends and neighbours: Annie, Connie, Carol, and Sue the librarian.

Naturally, she has incorporated into the strip many aspects of daily life in the North Bay area, much like she did while living in Lynn Lake. One of the most recognizable stories is of Elizabeth attending Nipissing University. The school was so thrilled by the acknowledgement and the publicity that they had a life-size "standee" made of Elizabeth. This colourful plywood character "attended" school with the other first-year education students and was photographed with the graduating class.

Nipissing University was mentioned regularly in the strip while Elizabeth studied there.

I'M GLAD YOU DON'T MIND DRIVING ME TO THE SCHOOL WITH YOU, GRETA.

NO PROBLEM. I'M GOING THERE ANYWAY! —AND, I LIKE THE COMPANY.

SEEMS STRANGE TO BE COMMUTING EVERY DAY TO THE TOWN I GREW UP IN. BUT, I MARRIED A GUY WHO WORKS IN NORTH BAY, SO....

I GREW UP IN GARDEN VILLAGE, JUST OUTSIDE STURGEON FALLS. IT'S A PRETTY PLACE. I COULD TAKE YOU THERE SOME-TIME.

I'D LIKE THAT.

WHAT BRINGS YOU ALL THE WAY UP HERE, ELIZABETH?

....THIS.

North Bay borders Nipissing First Nation, and the town of Garden Village is about a forty-five-minute drive from Nipissing University. This stretch of highway is instantly recognizable to locals.

THERE WERE HOOP DANCERS AND FANCY DANCERS,

AND WOMEN IN JINGLE DRESSES WEARING HAND-MADE MOCCASINS.

THE MEN JUMPED AND WHIRLED...AND, WHENEVER AN EAGLE FEATHER FELL, THE DANCING STOPPED.

THIS MEANT THAT SOMEWHERE AN ELDER OR A VETERAN HAD DIED....

THEIR SPIRIT WAS ACKNOWLEDGED AND HONORED.

The Nipissing First Nation powwow dancers and their beautiful regalia so inspired Lynn that she drew a whole series of strips featuring the people she met.

Having spent so much of her career living in small communities, Lynn has come to appreciate the support a small town has to offer.

If I had begun my job as a comic strip artist in a big southern city, I would not have survived as well as I did. Without the support and the safety net of home, I would have fallen into the publicity trap and become something others wanted me to be. I would have lost "who I am." Aside from confidence and encouragement, a small community gave me a healthy sense of self.

THE BUSINESS EVOLVES

Until Lynn moved to North Bay, the business aspect of creating a daily comic series was relatively straightforward. She would regularly send her work via courier to UPS in Kansas City, and once a month they would send her a paycheque in exchange. If she turned in her work late, which wasn't often, she would be charged a penalty fee for each day a strip was late. It was up to the syndicate to negotiate with the different newspapers that carried her strip. Her wage was based on a percentage of the overall income of the strip. As the number of newspapers carrying *For Better or For Worse* increased, so did her monthly wage.

Because North Bay had regular air service and was just an hour's flight from Toronto, I had more reason to accept invitations to speak, to market my books, and to see my editors at the syndicate. I loved to travel. I could sit on a quiet plane for several hours and read — guilt free. "Doing nothing" was a rare treat for me. I was always busy doing something. My life was divided up into time-slots: family, kids, social, work, work, and more work. I was driven by deadlines. I would get a huge amount done in a day because, in order to meet my deadlines, I had no choice — I had to produce. With all of the time I was spending away from home travelling, I soon realized that I needed help. I hired Karen Matchette, a talented artist who had worked for Hank Ketcham on *Dennis the Menace,* to help with the drawing of the strip.

Lynn had hired friends in the past to do some of the colouring of the Sunday pages and to answer fan mail, but never before had she trusted anyone to work on the drawing of the strip. To entice Karen and her family to move to North Bay from California, Lynn bought a house on the lake, just down the road from her own house, and rented it to Karen. It wasn't long before they had their routine down: Lynn would do all the rough drawing in pencil and draw the characters in ink; Karen would then draw in backgrounds and the lettering and apply the screentone (clear adhesive sheets covered in dotted patterns, which before Photoshop, gave black-and-white cartoons depth and texture).

> This worked like a charm. Karen was wonderful. Together we hit the deadlines at a reasonable pace. With Karen working full-time, I had more time for friends, family, and freedom.

Before long, Lynn hired another employee to answer the phone, help with bookkeeping, and do a variety of office jobs. Initially, the two women worked out of Lynn's basement studio space in the log house, and Lynn made a new spot for herself on the main floor, just off of the kitchen.

When Karen and her family returned to the States because her husband had difficulty finding work in the area, Lynn hired two local artists: a talented graphic designer and an expert computer colourist.

> I couldn't work with all these people coming into my house every day, so we built a lovely little studio on a piece of property across the road. For the first time in a long time, I was working outside of my house. With the four of us working together, we began to take on all kinds of projects aside from the strip. I did artwork for various non-profit groups in town, we did a series of little books, made calendars and greeting cards, and cover art for the collection books. We kept busy.

As time went on, Lynn hired more people: a full-time website developer, someone to "manage" the business, and eventually, another person as assistant manager. The expanded full-time staff quickly outgrew the little studio.

We sold the little studio building, and moved into the large, now renovated, house we'd bought for Karen. Rod hired another part-time person to do the mail, which added one more woman to the "team."

(above) It wasn't hard for Lynn to imagine Elly's trials as a business owner.

(left) Lynn enjoyed the view of a very small lake from her desk at this studio.

Rod had always taken an active role in Lynn's business — managing the books, helping make big decisions, providing material for the strip, and being a sounding board for Lynn. With new prospects on the horizon, Rod cut his dental practice down to part-time and began to co-manage Lynn's company, among other things.

Looking back, it seems crazy to have had so many staff members. For a job that I once did all by myself, I often wondered why we needed so many people. I was busy with the strip and the countless other projects that we had on the go; so as long as everyone was happy and we were paying the bills, I didn't question it. Together we produced a tremendous amount of stuff, and we sure had a lot of fun. It is pretty incredible that because of this job, I was able to provide some fabulous opportunities, as well as steady wages, to this group of talented people.

PERKS OF THE JOB

The life of a cartoonist is generally a solitary and lonely one, but through the strip, Lynn has been fortunate enough to travel widely. Over the years, it has been essential for Lynn to connect with her colleagues — to build friendships, compare notes, and, well, vent.

I needed other artists as much as I needed my editors and others at the syndicate in Kansas City. My connection to fellow cartoonists who laboured in basements, struggling with deadlines like I did, was essential.

Once a year the National Cartoonists Society (NCS), known as "the world's largest and most prestigious organization of professional cartoonists," puts on the Reuben Awards. This is a weekend-long event for members of the NCS to congregate, catch up on the past year, attend lectures and seminars, welcome new up-and-coming cartoonists, and, most importantly, enjoy a few drinks with good friends. The Reuben Award for Outstanding Cartoonist of the Year is presented at this event.

Through the NCS, and specifically, the Reuben weekend, Lynn has met many of her long-time childhood heroes. A few have become very close friends.

Every year the Reuben Awards, the "Oscars" of the comic art world, along with book fairs and comic art conventions, bring cartoonists together from all over the world. Travelling to these events became the highlight of my year and a regular family adventure. In 1986 I had the honour of winning the award. It was a surprise to me — I didn't feel as though I was ready. I thought Jim Davis should have won for *Garfield* that year. I shook as I accepted the statue. And I blushed when Charles Schulz, or "Sparky" (his childhood nickname, the name by which all of his close friends and family called him), said that he'd voted for me.

This wasn't the first time she had spoken with Sparky, but being acknowledged by someone whom she had looked up to for so long was difficult to get used to.

One day, very early in my career, the phone rang, and I ran to answer it.

A voice said, "Hello, this is Charles Schulz. I just wanted you to know that I like your work!"

Thinking it was a joke, I said, "Who?"

Rather apologetically he said, "I do *Peanuts*?" I had to sit down. He had asked Cathy Guisewite for my phone number and had called me at home. I couldn't believe it.

(top) A stunned-looking Lynn with her Reuben Award, 1986.
She was the first female and the first Canadian to win the award.

(bottom) Lynn rarely broke the "fourth wall" in her strip, since *For Better or For Worse* was so realistic, but she made exceptions for Charles and Jeannie Schulz.

Lynn and Sparky forged a long and caring friendship. Lynn acknowledges that meeting and getting to know Sparky and his wife, Jeannie, was a highlight in her career.

My friendships within this business are something I cherish. Cartoonists gravitate toward other cartoonists as do people in self-help groups who all share the same affliction! By reading into each other's work, there's a sense of already knowing that person long before you meet face to face.

Cathy Guisewite, Charles Schulz, and Lynn in LA at the Reuben Awards, 1992. Cathy won the Reuben that year.

Camaraderie certainly enriched Lynn's experience as a cartoonist, creating a sense of community among fellow artists.

I have so many great memories. I have known so many wonderful comic artists. We met at dinners and conventions, book signings, speaking engagements, and house-to-house visits. We have travelled together, seen each other's families grow, and we have attended the funerals of those who died. Cartoonists, for the most part, are funny, talented, sensitive, giving, and caring people. All are incredibly hard working — driven by deadlines and dreams. We have so much in common; we are all performers, writers, artists, and storytellers. It's taken me sixty years to accept and appreciate the skills we share. We are all uniquely gifted — something we accept but don't really understand. This makes us all a close-knit family. Since our syndicates compete

to get our work out there, we are free to enjoy each other's company without reservation: nobody hopes the other guy fails. If *Blondie* bumps *For Better or For Worse* off a comics page, I can still have dinner with Dean and Charlotte Young and not think about the number of papers we're in.

One time, Tom Wilson, the creator of *Ziggy*, was sick. He had been hospitalized and couldn't produce the strip. Jim Unger (*Herman*), Jim Davis (*Garfield*), and I were together that weekend, and we decided to draw *Ziggy* for Tom. We did manage to come up with some gags, but the drawing threw us all. How can a simple round-headed guy with a big nose be so hard to draw?!

As it turns out, our characters are like signatures. We each have our own particular scrawl, and to copy it takes time and patience. This told us [that] even though *Ziggy* is a competitor, we all loved Tom and wanted to do anything we could to make his life easier.

THE STRIP TAKES ON A LIFE OF ITS OWN

Not many cartoonists have had the success that Lynn has with *For Better or For Worse*. A contributing factor may be that Lynn has kept the characters and the strip growing. What began as a gag-a-day panel has evolved into a huge community of characters — personalities — that seem to exist somewhere in the universe and in the hearts of millions of fans. Lynn has put an inordinate amount of energy into adding fine details to her drawings and to her stories, making her fictional world realistic.

It wasn't until I did the animated shows that there was need for real continuity in the strip. I had to create an architectural drawing and floor plan of the Patterson house for the background artists, and this wasn't easy. I also needed a map of their town! When I created the strip, I didn't think that it would ever matter, so I had combined the exterior of our one-level Dundas house with the interior of our two-level house in Lynn Lake. It was an impossible layout, but we managed to sort it out, and fortunately, nobody pointed out the inconsistencies. I also drew an aerial view of the neighbourhood and the town where the Pattersons lived. This was extremely helpful in that it gave me a clear view of my own imaginary comic strip world. It was also the beginning of the "realification" of everything. This encouraged me to start drawing very realistic homes, furniture, cars, buildings, and people. My fast and easy flowing lines became much more controlled and each panel became a serious illustration. I wanted readers to see my characters' surroundings as clearly as I did. My graphic artist and colourist complained that when I drew a grocery store, for example, I'd draw everything on the shelves — including the labels!

The Pattersons' neighbourhood drawn as reference material
for a series of Lynn's animated shows.

From then on, everything I drew came from something I saw, experienced, felt, or knew to be true. I tried to make people look and act like people. I tried to make things look like things. I used toys, for example, to give me perspective on everything from cars to fridges to Rollerblades. One of the most useful toys I have is a small wire shopping cart. Try drawing a shopping cart from memory! I have toy animals, toy hats, and sports equipment. If there was a toy out there I could use to draw from, I bought it. Another great find was a miniature drum set, which I featured in April's band. I had an "*ah-hah* moment" when I discovered that toys made great drawing tools. This is one of the tricks of the trade that I enjoy sharing with young artists.

Lynn continued to look to her community for inspiration. People, places, stories — she never knew where her next idea would come from. In fact, she would carry a pen and paper with her at all times to jot down ideas as they came. If she didn't do this, the thought would be gone — forever.

Brad Luggsworth is a combination of bullies Lynn has known.

After the family had settled into North Bay, Lynn was forced to break the Patterson family away from the Johnstons. "I had always tried to protect my family's privacy, to not write about sensitive, personal things or to reveal any small truths unless I had their approval to do so," but Aaron and Kate were being bullied in school as a result of the strip. Lynn's status as a "local celebrity" wasn't helping matters. It was time for a change.

At this point, Lynn had gained such strong reader support that she felt she could push the storyline a little. With the help of Lee at UPS, she did just that.

From 1987 onward, lighter moments in the lives of the characters were balanced by more serious things. The strip dealt with real-world issues including political activism, alcoholism and child abuse, physical handicaps, the ego-crushing experience of being laid off, ethics in the press and — most controversial — the coming out of a gay teenager. The story of Michael Patterson's friend Lawrence coming out has been one of Lynn's most poignant storylines. She was moved to do this story after the news that her high school friend Michael VadeBoncoeur had died.

I was walking into my studio when the strangest sensation occurred. I suddenly thought about my friend Michael. I called him, but there was no answer at his apartment. I then called our friend Paul. He told me that Michael had been murdered by a young man he had befriended. The intruder took Michael's bicycle and his stereo after having slit his throat. I was devastated. The news reported a brief story about a Canadian comedy writer being killed. The feeling I had from the way his death was reported was that this was just another gay man who got what he deserved.

As was everyone who knew this kind, talented, funny man, I was in shock. I wanted, in some way, to say out loud that this wasn't the death of a gay man; it was the death of my childhood friend. Someone I knew and had worked with and cared about. I called Lee at the syndicate and asked if I could do a story about a gay teenager coming out. He thought it would be provocative and that I might lose a few papers, but if I did it well, now was a good time for a story like this.

Lynn received thousands of handwritten letters — so many that she had boxes (separated into two piles: positive responses and negative responses) lining the walls of her studio. The positive responses heavily outweighed the negative. Even today, twelve years later, she has a fairly regular stream of comments about the "Lawrence story" and requests to reprint the saga, at least in part.

The second most "popular" storyline was, of course, the death of Farley the dog. As upset as people were to see this loveable character die, his death made the strip feel that much more real to readers. Lynn still misses the character Farley. His antics were often based on Lynn's black cocker spaniel Willy, who came into her life shortly after she moved to North Bay. Farley was believable, unlike most cartoon dog characters of his day. He was cute and loveable, and he will forever be the most beloved character in *For Better or For Worse*.

With her new format of taking from the world around her, Lynn introduced more characters of varying ethnic backgrounds and cultures. She wanted her fictional city to be similar to her own world and the people who inhabited it. Occasionally, she based a number of these characters on her friends. The inclusiveness of the strip has definitely contributed to its appeal and its ever-growing fan base.

Canadians are all colours, shapes, and sizes, and I wanted to show, with respect and honesty, . . . the diversity, which is all around us. In doing so, I received some kind comments from readers. The one, which remains foremost in my mind, is a letter from a young Iranian woman who thanked me for showing a girl in a hijab waiting to order a coffee in a corner café. She didn't have a speaking part, she was just a girl in line. The letter said, "Thanks for saying I exist." I wanted the challenge of drawing faces that weren't reflected in my mirror but were reflected in my world.

The response Lynn has received over the span of her career has been overwhelming: some of the letters were heartwarming, others expressed unbelievable pain and sorrow, and some were just plain weird. Some of Lynn's readers even came to have very real feelings toward the characters. She has received letters and emails from people who have wanted to marry Elizabeth, Michael, or Grandpa Jim. Occasionally, a note would be accompanied by photos.

LISTEN, EVERYONE — I'VE DIVIDED OUR CLASS INTO 6 GROUPS!

EACH GROUP HAS 4 PEOPLE IN IT, AND EACH GROUP IS REPRESENTED BY A DIFFERENT COLOR.

WHAT GROUP ARE YOU IN?

BLUE GROUP!

ME TOO!

THIS IS COOL, DUNCAN. — WE'RE BOTH THE SAME COLOR!!

When Grandpa Jim was single and talking about loneliness, a lady from Michigan wrote to say she was single, available, and would love to meet him! She said she was youthful and fun-loving and enclosed in her letter was a photograph of herself in a pink bunny suit. It was sweet! We all wished we could play cupid and introduce the two.

In another instance, before the advent of Facebook and Twitter, Michael Patterson was about to become engaged to Deanna Sobinski, when a letter arrived from a female fan. She demanded that before Michael got married he had to meet her first! She said how much she disliked Deanna and how wrong she was for Michael. At first, we thought the letter was a joke, but reading it again made us realize this young woman was quite serious. We could have created a dating service using the funny pages!

Over and over again, we were all impressed by how seriously the readers related to the characters and storylines. As the strip matured, I had to be careful not to alienate people who were reading more into my work than was intended. Writing sometimes went from being a fun challenge to being a serious responsibility. To many, both the characters and the storylines were real. I think this happens in television series as well; I know — I didn't want *The Mary Tyler Moore Show* to end!

Cartoonists, like anyone else, have a "boss." For Lynn's comic strip, the boss was Universal Press Syndicate; for her books it was Andrews McMeel Publishing.

It's hard to take criticism from someone whose opinion you don't respect. Lee Salem, Sue Roush, and Dorothy O'Brien kept me in line for thirty years, while giving me the most incredible freedom to develop *For Better or For Worse* in my own way. If I thought I might be pushing the envelope, I'd call and go over a storyline with them. No point in sending in work if there was a possibility it might be rejected.

It was Lee who encouraged me to do the Lawrence story, and he was right there with me when Farley the dog died. Neither of us expected these two storylines to elicit such an emotional response. If there was ever any question regarding the content of my strip, Lee was always supportive.

Sue has been my resource for correct word use, punctuation, spelling, and dialogue. She has approved all my "Canadianisms" and has checked continuity in drawing and content and has made me think twice on a number of occasions about a drawing or a thought.

Dorothy has advised me on content, overseen the production, and edited all of my books. I have been guided, and sometimes saved, by my editors and have never thanked them enough!

Thank you for being part of my Success. Without your support and continuing faith in what I do, I would not have the honor of writing this message to you today. I am so fortunate to be working with you and for you.
Yours Sincerely...

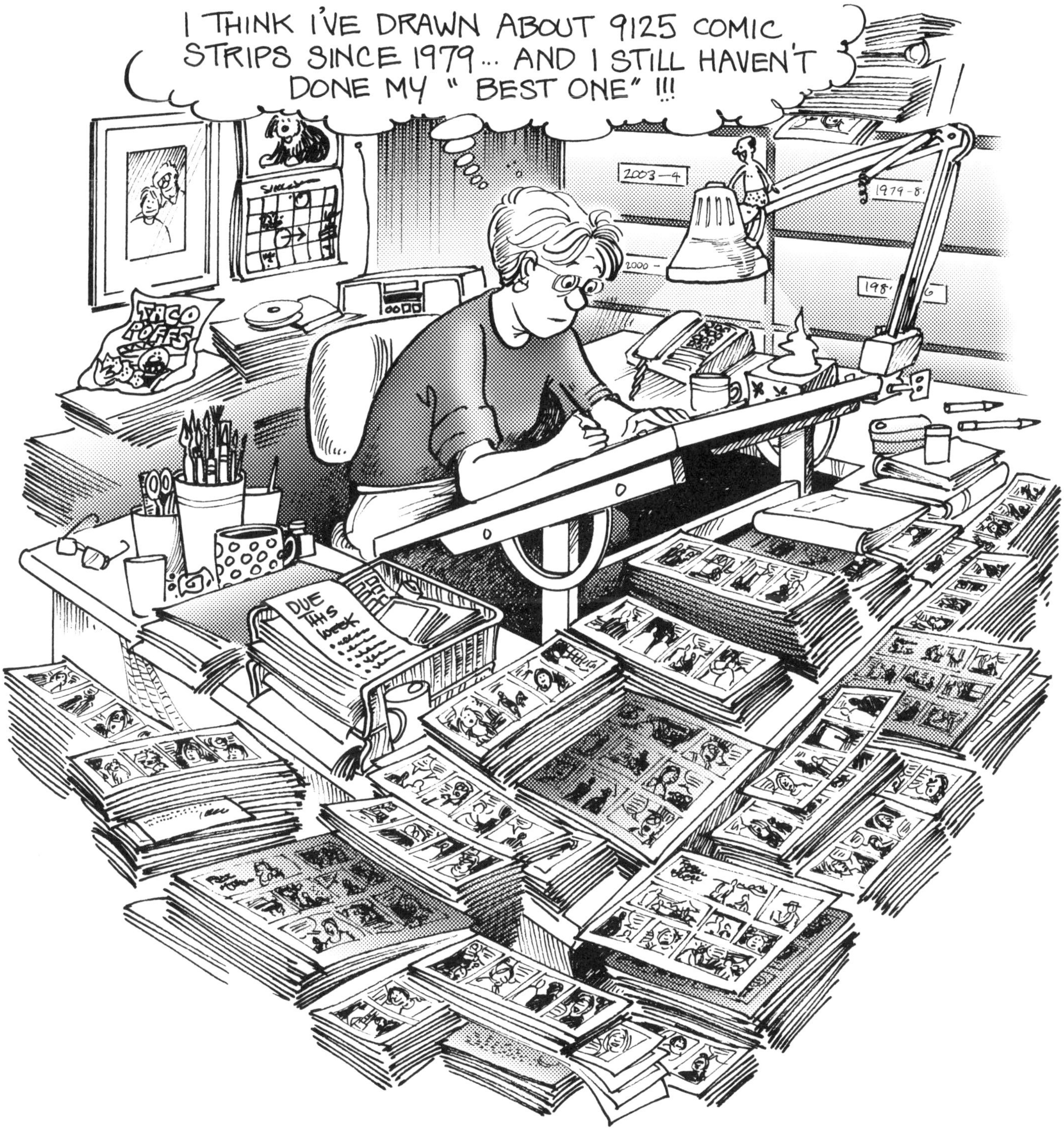
I THINK I'VE DRAWN ABOUT 9125 COMIC STRIPS SINCE 1979... AND I STILL HAVEN'T DONE MY "BEST ONE" !!!
DUE THIS WEEK
TACO PUFFS
2003-4
1979-8
2000

This image was drawn for the inside of the book *Suddenly Silver*, which celebrated the strip's twenty-fifth anniversary, in 2004.

After nearly thirty years of writing *For Better or For Worse*, the story of the Patterson family was going to end. Lynn was reaching retirement age and was looking forward to life with no deadlines. She wanted to try her hand at painting.

With the large number of characters and the many storylines within the story, Lynn had to plan to wrap up the strip years before it actually ended. The readers certainly didn't want to see the story end; it had become a regular part of their lives. The prospect of an end to the strip posed a tremendous personal, emotional, and psychological loss for Lynn, too: "I don't think that anyone really takes the time to think about how difficult it is to write and create and produce a column like this."

There were a number of reasons that made the timing perfect for Lynn to end the strip. The story had naturally begun again: Elly and John's children had become adults with kids of their own. Lynn's "real" children were both living on the West Coast of Canada and had lives of their own. Grandchildren were just a passing thought.

It was not the same as having young children around for inspiration.
I began to struggle to connect with the language and the mannerisms
of young people today.

By now Charles Schulz had died. He had been her mentor, her friend, and her hero. Besides her editors, Schulz was the one person in the industry she looked to for approval. He was a father figure. Lynn acknowledges, "When he died, a spark in me died too."

The information age was here. The Internet was changing the way people got their news, communicated with each other, and read the comics. One by one, newspapers were shutting down, unable to compete with the free information online. It was beginning to look as though newspapers and books would one day be obsolete. There was considerable fear in the industry about what was going to happen. A lot of unknown factors were at play, and it was anybody's guess as to what the future held for the comics page.

Lynn had a well-established website. She was receiving daily messages from her fans through the Web. Handwritten letters seemed to be a thing of the past. The phenomenon of instant feedback had a strong impact on Lynn.

> Along with the emails from the usual fans came the would-be writers who tried to guess how the strip would end. They came up with every possible conclusion, and of course, one of them was right. I stopped reading their online discussions long before I wrote the final chapter. I knew that no matter how close they came to guessing, my ending would still be my own idea, my own dialogue, my own scenarios — and in my own time. Nonetheless, they took some of the joy away. They sapped some of the excitement. Now, when I look at the way the online critics and the "end guessers" affected me, I wonder how the next generation of creative and talented artists is going to be able to share their gifts with the world, if they, and their creations, are attacked at every turn.

There is another group of people that Lynn and her staff have come to call "the snarkers." They appear to be a relatively small group, but they proved to be quite destructive and distracting. They take pride in combing through the years and years of strips, looking for inconsistencies and errors, and then happily point out their findings online.

> As a panic- and deadline-driven new comic strip creator, I cared more about the gags (if I was lucky) and the drawings (if I was sharp) than recording birth dates and other time-identifying landmarks. I had no idea that this kind of stuff would ever be important! Nor did I think there would come a time when explaining who the characters were, how they came together, and what had shaped their personalities would be of interest to anyone but me.

What is fascinating is that "the snarkers" consider themselves fans — super-fans — but they don't seem to realize there is a person with real feelings behind the work.

At a comic art event in Pittsburgh in 2013, I was asked what made me stop writing the strip. I gave the usual reasons: I felt the story had ended and I was afraid to let the work decline, so best to end the story while it was still popular. But one of the reasons I had not revealed was my anger and frustration with trolls, snarkers — whatever you want to call these folks — who love to send out mean, cruel, and totally useless criticism about everything you do. Anonymously, they tear your work to shreds, and if you respond they feel rewarded. If you ignore them, they are undeterred.

It was evident there was no way to please everyone, so why even try.

I look at my work every day and wish it was funnier, better drawn, more meaningful, but it's the best I can do and it's part of me. It's a story that's grown from rough sketches and four-panel gags to something beyond my control.

Despite what anyone was saying online, it did not detract from the success of *For Better or For Worse.* But it was time for the strip to end.

In fact, Lynn and her staff knew seven years in advance that the strip would be ending. For those seven years, the work continued. Lynn kept producing the strip every day. Together they tied up loose storylines and tried to figure out how to keep the company running after *For Better or For Worse* ended. With all the talent housed in Lynn's studio and all the projects the staff worked on, the strip was the only thing that generated an income. At the time, Lynn believed they had all the right people with all the right skills to start a great advertising agency, and she felt the community could support such a business. All they needed was someone to take the bull by the horns and get it done. No one jumped at the opportunity.

Things were beginning to get tense at Lynn's studio. As the end crept closer, the tension grew stronger. With uncertainty about their jobs and the prospect of finding alternative employment, the staff grew anxious. Making matters worse, a rift between the staff developed when the executive team began turning the company's focus to investing and real estate. Neglecting the business of the comic strip, and other creative aspects of the business, made the art department and the design staff feel neglected and undervalued. On top of all of that, Lynn sensed there was something more going on — but what?

> I was starting to realize that my business had gotten out of my control. Meetings about the direction of my company didn't include me — even though I was the sole breadwinner. I was under a tremendous amount of stress at the time, and I admit that I was becoming very forgetful. My husband told me that I had Alzheimer's and Parkinson's disease, and would eventually have to be put in a home. If this wasn't bad enough, he told my staff and other people in the community this "news," too. Every time I forgot my keys or left a door unlocked, it was a sign of senility.

I went to a neurologist and was told I was healthy but suffering from anxiety. Rod and a number of my staff didn't believe this. I, too, began to doubt my own sanity.

Around 2001, Lynn discovered she had spasmodic torticollis, a form of the movement disorder known as dystonia. In her case, her head twists and turns uncontrollably to the left when she lies down. The disorder is made worse by anxiety.

My muscles twisted with the strength it takes to wring out a wet towel. I was told by my local doctor that my symptoms were psychosomatic. If this was the case then why was I miserable all night long? I wasn't looking for attention. My bed became my enemy. I couldn't sleep lying down, so I began to sleep sitting up in a chair.

When I was properly diagnosed by a neurologist, I contacted a dystonia hotline and discovered how prevalent and incapacitating these kinds of disorders are. I helped to fundraise for dystonia awareness and in doing so, I heard stories much like my own. I have taken medication, tried Botox and massage, but relief was not to be had. With work and other stresses weighing me down, the pain became unbearable.

Things seemed to go from bad to worse. A kind of sickness invaded the studio. Aside from Lynn's personal issues, the staff detected an inexplicable tension within the "management" team.

Rod and the company's executive director had convinced my staff that I was senile, unstable, and not interested in knowing what was going on within the business. Because of the tension, people picked at each other and treated me as though I would explode at any time. With deadlines continually nagging at me, all I could do was put my head down and get the strip done. Eventually, we discovered the source of the unease: my husband had been having an affair with the executive director, the woman he'd hired to run my business. It was a shock. When it was out, the affair was over. So was the marriage.

The discovery caused a huge rift in Lynn's business. The staff divided along lines of loyalty: those who were faithful to Rod as their boss and those who were faithful to Lynn. Lynn's personal life was in shambles, and now her business was, too. On a personal level, she found it too painful to draw John because John, in many ways, was Rod — at least from Lynn's perspective. It was terribly difficult to think of John as the loving, supportive spouse he had evolved into from his early days as a bumbling, socially awkward chauvinist. This didn't go unnoticed to her detail-catching fans.

In 2007 Lynn and Rod were divorced. The support of her children, as well as her friends and family, saw Lynn through a difficult and painful period. Upon hearing the news of the affair, Aaron had dropped everything and headed home. After tying up loose ends, and packing up her apartment in Vancouver, Kate soon returned home, too. With Lynn's world turned upside down, she and her kids worked together to sort out everything in her personal life and in the business. It was an awful time for everyone.

The one thing that calmed my nerves, strangely enough, was to lie on the floor and scream. Vodka helped, too. I can see why some people drink too much — it helps to deaden the pain.

By now Lynn was down to a skeleton crew at the studio, which was easier in many ways. Kate did her best to fill in where she could. With the end of the strip in sight, Lynn spent the next year wrapping up ongoing plots, doing her best to see the characters settled on their paths and to come up with a good ending for the strip because, "a story is only as good as its ending."

IRIS, YOU'VE TAKEN SUCH GOOD CARE OF GRANDPA JIM. HE'S SO LUCKY TO HAVE YOU!

WE'RE BOTH LUCKY, DEAR.

BUT, SO MANY THINGS HE CAN'T DO FOR HIMSELF NOW - AND YOU'RE WITH HIM, LOOKING AFTER HIM DAY AFTER DAY ... IT CAN'T BE EASY!

IT'S NOT EASY.

BUT WE MADE A COMMITMENT - JUST AS YOU DID TODAY - AND ALTHOUGH IT'S NOT EASY, THIS IS ALL PART OF LOVING SOMEONE - WITH ALL YOUR HEART ... AND, WITH ALL YOU HAVE TO GIVE!

IT'S A PROMISE THAT SHOULD LAST A LIFETIME. IT DEFINES YOU AS A PERSON AND DESCRIBES YOUR SOUL. IT'S A PROMISE TO BE THERE, ONE FOR THE OTHER, NO MATTER WHAT HAPPENS, NO MATTER WHO FALLS ...

FOR BETTER OR FOR WORSE, MY DEARS ... FOR BETTER OR FOR WORSE.

THIS CONCLUDES MY STORY.... WITH GRATEFUL THANKS TO EVERYONE WHO HAS MADE THIS ALL POSSIBLE ~ Lynn Johnston

Since not all of the newspapers carried both the daily and the Sunday comics,
Lynn had to draw two final strips. This is the final daily, published on August 30, 2008.

For almost thirty years, I lived in a comic-strip world. People and places existed in my head and things happened on schedule according to dates and deadlines. I lived in the parallel world of *For Better or For Worse* until the saga ended with the marriage of the Pattersons' eldest daughter, Elizabeth, to her longtime friend Anthony Caine. Normally one wraps up a story and it's done. But I was offered the opportunity to see my work appear a second time in the newspapers, and after the initial overwhelming surprise, a kind of panic set in.

Lynn's syndicate wasn't willing to let *For Better or For Worse* go entirely, and three decades of material meant there was a generation who hadn't yet read the entire strip. Lynn and the staff at UPS worked out a way to run the strip again from the beginning.

Lynn included occasional flashbacks to older strips within the current strips to introduce the original material, so people could get to know the characters as they were in the '80s. The syndicate started blending in weeks of old strips with the new material, and after the final *For Better or For Worse* strip ran in August 2008, readers opened their newspapers the next day to find Lynn's work was still on the comics page.

The use of flashbacks to transition readers to reading the comic from the beginning again had never been done before. No one really knew how it was going to be received. Time has proven the strategy worked: Lynn has maintained her fan base and her readership, and her business is carrying on.

152

DADDY, WHO'S THIS?

THAT'S GRAND-PA JIM, YOUR GREAT-GRAND-FATHER.

AND WHO'S THIS LADY?

GRANDMA MARIAN. SHE DIED BEFORE YOU WERE BORN.

I NEVER SAW HER?

NO—AND I DIDN'T SEE HER MUCH, EITHER. SHE AND GRANDPA JIM LIVED ON THE OTHER SIDE OF THE COUNTRY.

WHY DID THEY MOVE SO FAR AWAY?

THEY DIDN'T. THEIR DAUGHTER-YOUR GRANDMA ELLY-MOVED HERE TO GO TO SCHOOL.

IT'S SORT OF A LONG STORY!

THAT'S OK, DADDY. ...I'VE GOT TIME.

SO GRAMMA ELLY AND GRAMPA JOHN GOT MARRIED?

AFTER A WHILE THEY DID.

DAD HAD A COUPLE MORE YEARS TO GO BEFORE HE GRADUATED, AND MOM WAS ONLY IN FIRST YEAR. AFTER A FEW MONTHS, MOM LEFT SCHOOL AND STARTED WORKING SO THEY COULD SAVE SOME MONEY.

AND THEN THEY HAD YOU?

NO! THEY GOT MARRIED FIRST...

...AND I WAS A BIT OF A SURPRISE.

HONESTLY, I DON'T KNOW **HOW** IT HAPPENED!!

A sample of strips from Lynn's flashback period.

AT FIRST, I WAS REALLY JEALOUS OF MY LITTLE SISTER. I WANTED EVERY-THING SHE HAD.

Y'KNOW, 'LIZABETH... YOU DON'T HAVE SUCH A GREAT LIFE AFTER ALL....

This strip originally ran on September 27, 1979
(minus the additional text in the first panel).

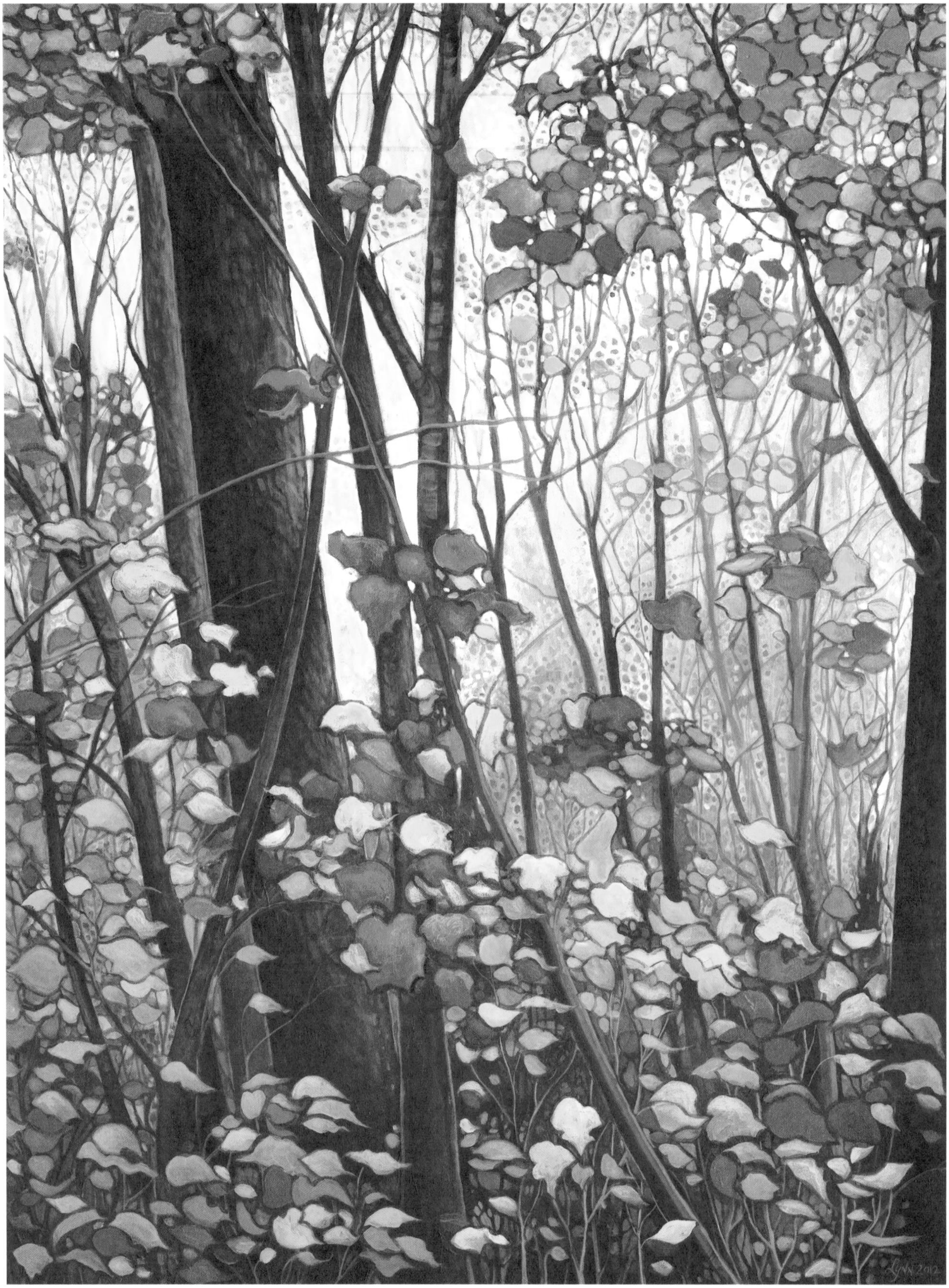
Lynn 2012

THAT'S A WRAP! OR IS IT A DRESS?

Since 2008 Lynn has dabbled in retirement. She threw herself a giant retirement party, complete with a live band, dancing, and food galore. People came from all over to attend the event: family and friends from across the country, cartoonist friends from here and there, even Lee Salem and Sue Roush came all the way from Kansas to celebrate the beginning of Lynn's freedom from the strip. The party was such a success that it became an annual event.

For someone who has lived with relentless deadlines her entire career, it was difficult for Lynn to slow down and get into retirement mode. She had wanted to try painting to get away from the tedium of drawing line cartoons, perhaps work in other mediums and create realistic imagery for a change.

> I love the feel, smell, and taste of acrylic, oil, and watercolour. I turned a spare bedroom into my "painting room" and filled it with all of the things that I needed to paint. There is an easel and a cabinet full of paints and brushes. Blank canvases line the walls of the room. I have done a few pieces. Some of them I am happy with. The thing is, I can't take serious images seriously. I like to use colour and line, but I have learned that the subject matter has to make me laugh or I lose interest.

(facing page) Lynn's favourite painting so far: *Forest*, acrylic on canvas, 2013, 76 x 102 cm.

(right) Lynn in her painting studio with granddaughter Laura, 2012.

By 2010 Lynn's life had drastically changed from a few years prior. She was partially retired and on her own. "I thought I'd settle in to a life of painting, reading, gardening, and, if I was lucky, grand-parenting, when the time came." The business was once again being run out of a small studio in Lynn's new lakeside home. Kate, now married, was living down the road from Lynn.

> Kate and I live a short five-minute walk from each other, which is wonderful. With a degree in fine arts and her ability to manage, Kate agreed to help me reorganize my work and my studio. In so doing, she began to sort through all of my projects, all of the accumulated flotsam of a thirty-year career.

Tucked away in Lynn's garage was a mind-boggling amount of paper and art she had stored. When the strip began, Rod's father obsessively collected newspaper clippings of *For Better or For Worse* and any interviews and articles about Lynn he could get his hands on. He carefully catalogued and scrapbooked these documents. These were stashed in ordinary cardboard boxes, along with scrapbooks her mother had assembled of Lynn's childhood art and samples of Lynn's graphic art before her UPS contract, among other treasures — including most of the original *For Better or For Worse* strips (a few had been sold or given away). With humidity and non-acid-free storage containers, some items were beginning to show signs of damage. Luckily most of the artwork was still in good shape. This discovery prompted Kate and Lynn to begin the process of scanning and preserving these materials. Thanks to the help of Lynn's web designer, Stephanie van Doleweerd, and her partner, Greg Wotton, this daunting task is almost complete.

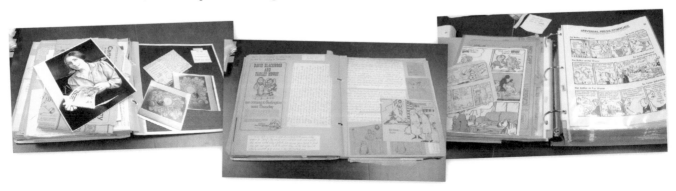

Examples of Lynn's scrapbooks that are being reassembled
using proper archival materials.

> In my closet Kate discovered a dress that I had worn when I was awarded a star on Canada's Walk of Fame in Toronto in 2003. It was an honour for me to receive such an award, and naturally, I worried about what to wear. I figured as a cartoonist, I should wear something fun, but I just couldn't find what I was looking for. So, I bought a plain

white wrap-around wedding dress, and with gooey squeezable fabric paint, I covered the lower half of the dress with cartoon faces. It was a hit. Throughout the evening, people asked me, "Where did you find that dress?!" They couldn't believe I had drawn all over a wedding dress.

Knowing this fabric paint was not meant to last forever, Kate decided the images should be digitized. It took some time to scan and digitally stitch the images together, but when the process was finished, she had a neat piece of art that could be enlarged or reduced or multiplied. This opened up an interesting area of design Lynn had not explored before. Excitement started to build around the business again, and ideas began to flow. Lynn, still interested in painting, started a series of small, funny acrylic animal paintings. These were scanned with the hope the images could be used on everything from notebooks, to mugs, to who knows what.

(above) Lynn's entire doodle on her "Funny Faces" dress — the result of scanning the dress and digitally stitching it together.

(left) Lynn in the middle of drawing on her dress with fabric "squeezy" paint.

(right) Lynn in her "Funny Faces" dress at an event in Vancouver, 2013.

First of a series of fun animal paintings that Lynn experimented with: *Funny Dog*, acrylic on canvas, 2013, 12 x 20 cm.

In 2014, after quite a bit of trial and error, the process that proved to offer the best result was when Lynn drew collages in ink on paper, Kate scanned them, and Lynn's graphic artist, Kevin Strang, coloured them digitally. So much for retirement! Lynn was now happily back at her drafting table — this time without the deadlines.

> Thinking this was a nifty idea, I began to make more funny designs, fish, cats, dogs, zoo animals — the possibilities are endless. With the help of Kate and Kevin, the designs have been expanded. There is no limit, in a digital age, to the number of variations that can be generated by one black–and–white design. Creating these doodle-like patterns has gone beyond a hobby. I just don't know where to take them next!

A whole new project started when Lynn had begun to think funny fashion wear might just be the right place for her patterns. Like any other exciting prospect, Lynn mentioned her ideas in passing to her friends. One of these people was Kathryn Brenne, a professional seamstress and fashion designer and a fellow dental wife. Kathryn saw real potential in what Lynn was doing, and together they came up with a plan to design some suitable prototype clothing using Lynn's funky patterns.

One of Lynn's new pattern designs. Lynn is planning on using
this particular zoo animal design on men's shirts and neckties.

Eight individual bird canvasses that Lynn and her staff were hoping would be photographed or scanned and reproduced on fabric, mugs, and other items. The texture of the canvas they were painted on made it difficult to make a clear digital reproduction: *Funny Birds*, acrylic on canvas, 2013, 8 x 8 cm each.

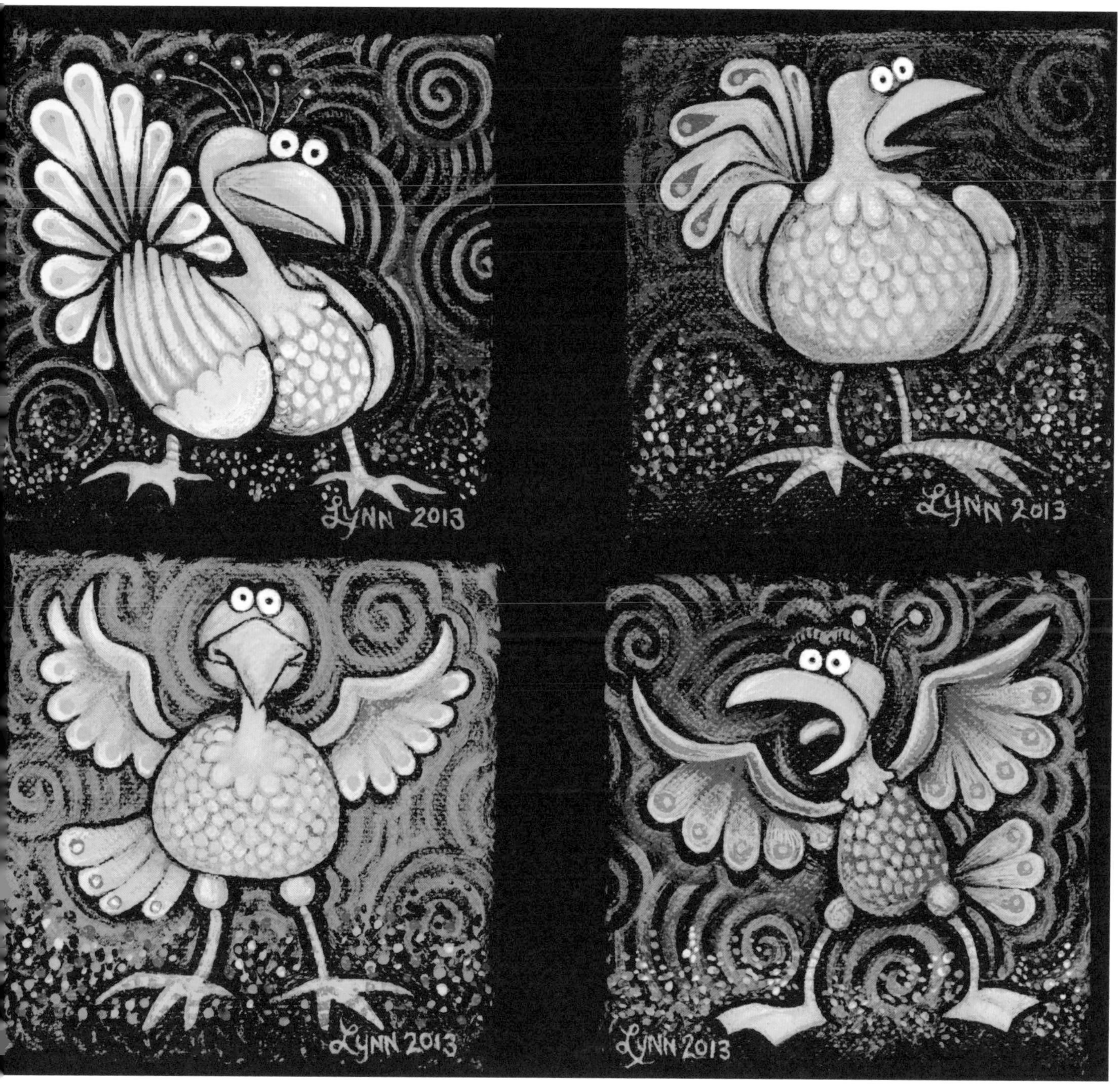
LYNN 2013
LYNN 2013
LYNN 2013
LYNN 2013

We just have prototypes at the moment: ties, dresses, children's and men's wear. We are putting them out into the world to see what happens. I never get involved in a project that I don't think will be successful, and I always do my best. If it doesn't take off, then I will still have a pretty neat pair of PJs to show for it.

I have had many doors opened for me during my lifetime. With the help of co-workers, family, publishers, serendipity, and friends, I have had opportunities galore. I have learned so much, and like others who have learned, accomplished, and achieved, I hope to open doors for others. In this ever-changing technological age, I look forward to seeing what's on the other side.

(top) A sample of a dress made by Kathryn Brenne's apprentice Malia Janveaux, using the "Fish Pattern," 2015.

(bottom) "Fish Pattern" in detail.

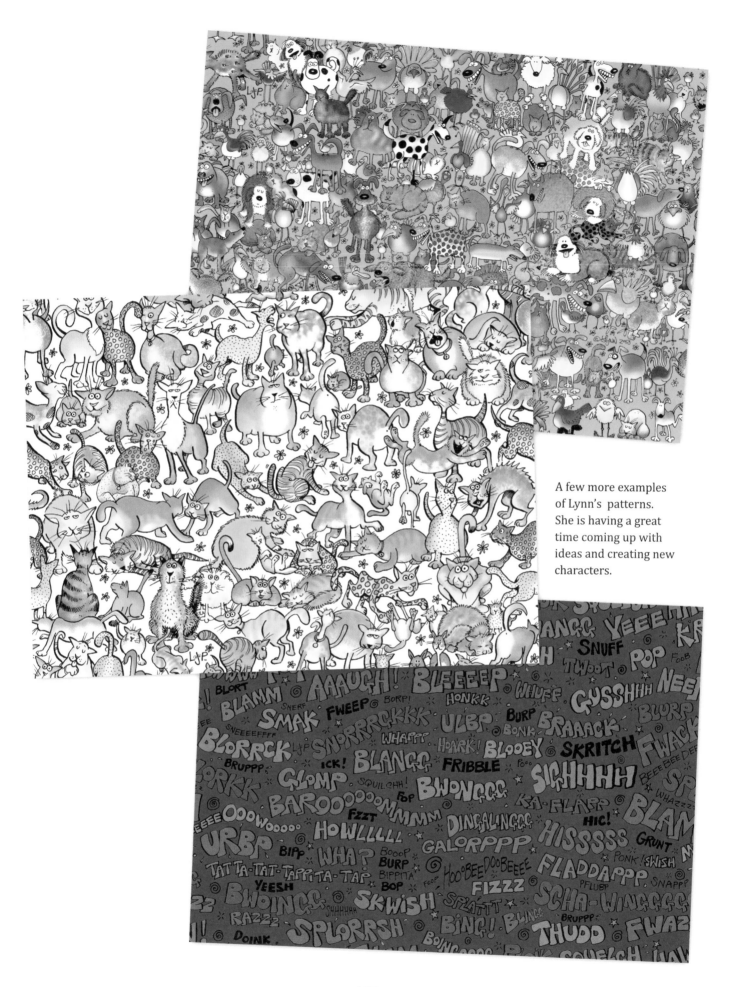

A few more examples of Lynn's patterns. She is having a great time coming up with ideas and creating new characters.

Despite the bumps in the road, I have had a great life. I've had a great career, met many wonderful people, and raised two beautiful children. I have two grandchildren, who fill my world with joy and comedy, and a renewed sense of wonder in everything around me. Life is, again, filled with fun and creativity. Despite all that has happened, for better or for worse, I can honestly say I have been very, very fortunate.

Lynn's most recent self-portrait, 2015. Drawing has become a challenge as vision problems and an essential tremor make it difficult for her to draw like she used to.

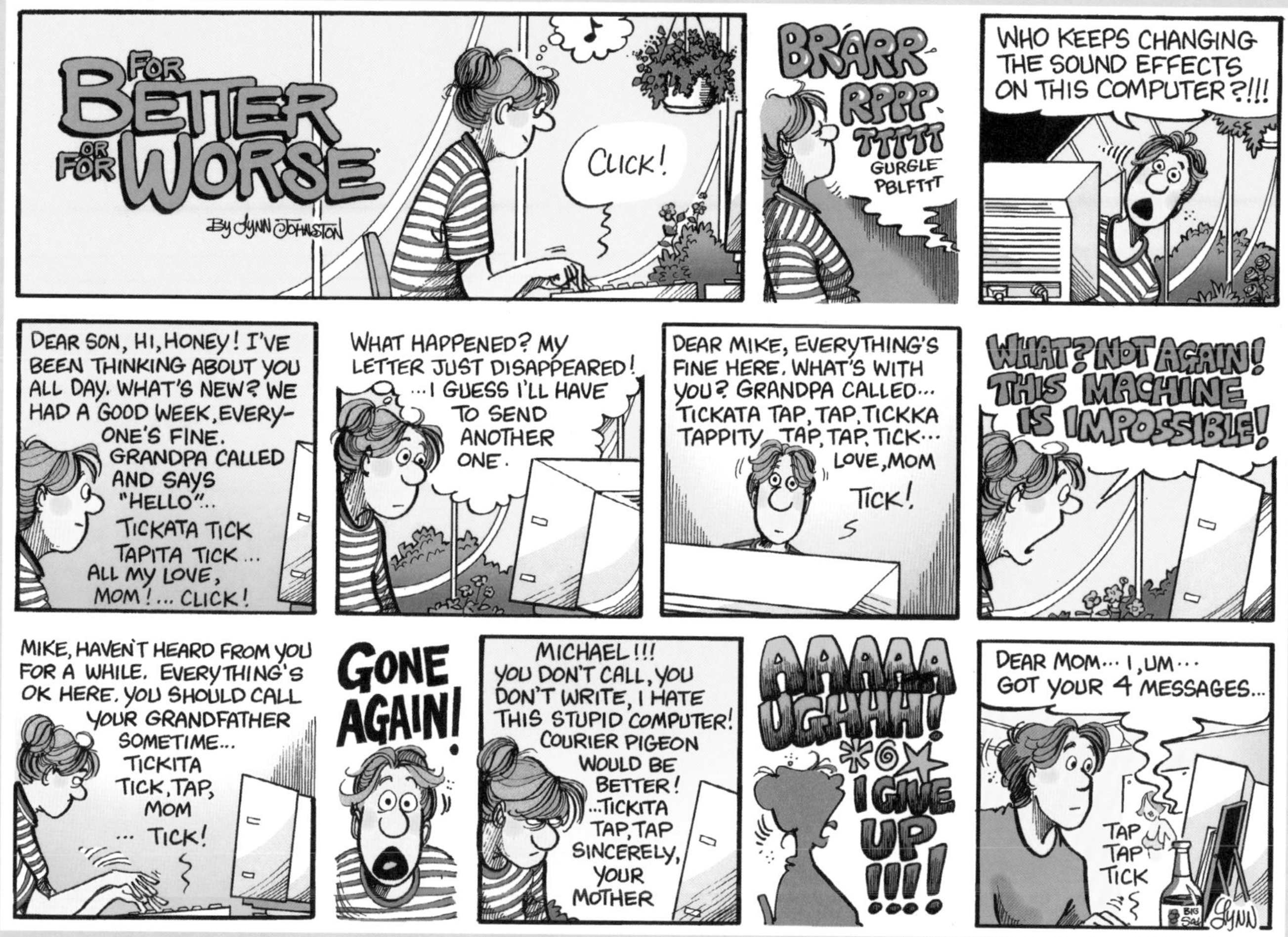
FOR BETTER OR FOR WORSE
BY LYNN JOHNSTON
CLICK!
BRARR RPPP TTTTT GURGLE PBLFTTT
WHO KEEPS CHANGING THE SOUND EFFECTS ON THIS COMPUTER?!!!
DEAR SON, HI, HONEY! I'VE BEEN THINKING ABOUT YOU ALL DAY. WHAT'S NEW? WE HAD A GOOD WEEK, EVERY-ONE'S FINE. GRANDPA CALLED AND SAYS "HELLO"... TICKATA TICK TAPITA TICK... ALL MY LOVE, MOM!... CLICK!
WHAT HAPPENED? MY LETTER JUST DISAPPEARED!
...I GUESS I'LL HAVE TO SEND ANOTHER ONE.
DEAR MIKE, EVERYTHING'S FINE HERE. WHAT'S WITH YOU? GRANDPA CALLED... TICKATA TAP, TAP, TICKKA TAPPITY TAP, TAP, TICK... LOVE, MOM
TICK!
WHAT? NOT AGAIN! THIS MACHINE IS IMPOSSIBLE!
MIKE, HAVEN'T HEARD FROM YOU FOR A WHILE. EVERYTHING'S OK HERE. YOU SHOULD CALL YOUR GRANDFATHER SOMETIME... TICKITA TICK, TAP, MOM ... TICK!
GONE AGAIN!
MICHAEL!!! YOU DON'T CALL, YOU DON'T WRITE, I HATE THIS STUPID COMPUTER! COURIER PIGEON WOULD BE BETTER! ...TICKITA TAP, TAP SINCERELY, YOUR MOTHER
AAAAA UGHHH! I GIVE UP!!!!
DEAR MOM... I, UM... GOT YOUR 4 MESSAGES...
TAP TAP TICK
LYNN

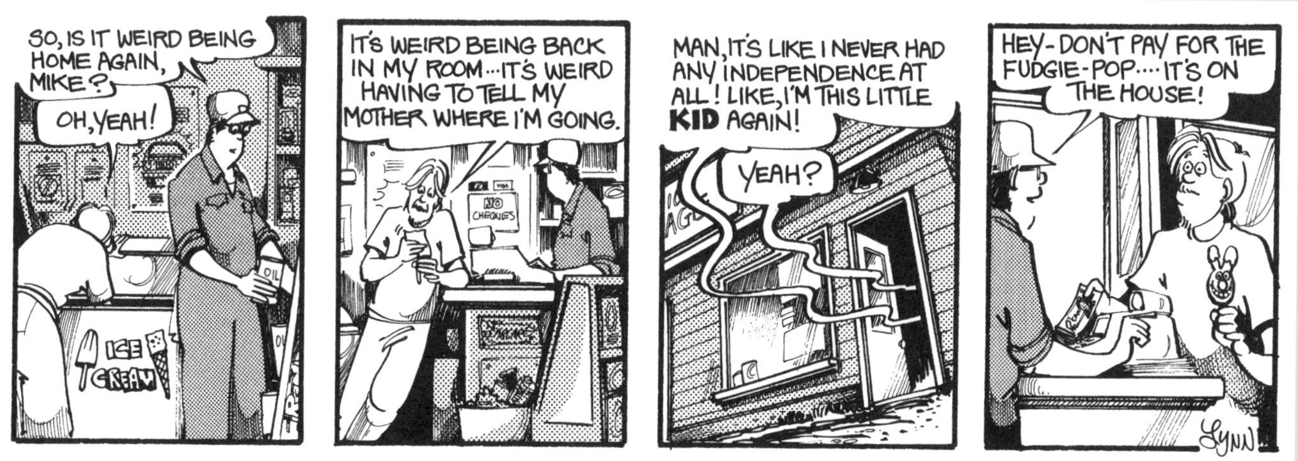
SO, IS IT WEIRD BEING HOME AGAIN, MIKE?
OH, YEAH!
ICE CREAM
IT'S WEIRD BEING BACK IN MY ROOM... IT'S WEIRD HAVING TO TELL MY MOTHER WHERE I'M GOING.
NO CHEQUES
MAN, IT'S LIKE I NEVER HAD ANY INDEPENDENCE AT ALL! LIKE, I'M THIS LITTLE **KID** AGAIN!
YEAH?
HEY- DON'T PAY FOR THE FUDGIE-POP.... IT'S ON THE HOUSE!
LYNN

NICKNAMES ARE OK, LIZ— THEY'RE TERMS OF ENDEARMENT.

THEY'RE TERMS OF WAR!

STÉPHANE, HOW'D YOU GET TO BE CALLED "SPUD"?

STÉPHANE PIERRE ULRIQUE DUPUIS. ...."SPUD".

WHERE DID "WEAZEL" COME FROM?

I HAD ASTHMA WHEN I WAS A KID AN' I USED TO WHEEZE ALL THE TIME, SO MY BROTHERS CALLED ME WEAZEL.

OPAL? WHAT DID YOU GET CALLED?

THE FAMILY JEWEL.

FOR Better OR FOR WORSE

By Lynn Johnston

RRRinngg!

HELLO?!!

ELIZABETH?— IT'S MOM!

OH, HI!

SO, WHAT'S UP?

JUST STUDY-ING.

ARE YOU DOING ANYTHING ON THE WEEKEND?

NOT MUCH

MET ANY NEW PEOPLE ON CAMPUS?

A FEW.

AND THAT NICE YOUNG MAN YOU MET ON THE BUS?

I'VE SEEN HIM AROUND.

HOW'S YOUR SOCIAL LIFE?

SO-SO.

IT'S BEEN NICE TALKING TO YOU HONEY.— I LOVE YOU!

YOU TOO, MOM

SIGH ELIZABETH TELLS ME WHAT'S GOING ON AT SCHOOL, BUT WHEN I ASK ABOUT HER LOVE LIFE, SHE TELLS ME NOTHING AT ALL.

WELL— YOU KNOW WHAT THEY SAY....

IF AT FIRST YOU DON'T SUCCEED... PRY, PRY AGAIN!!

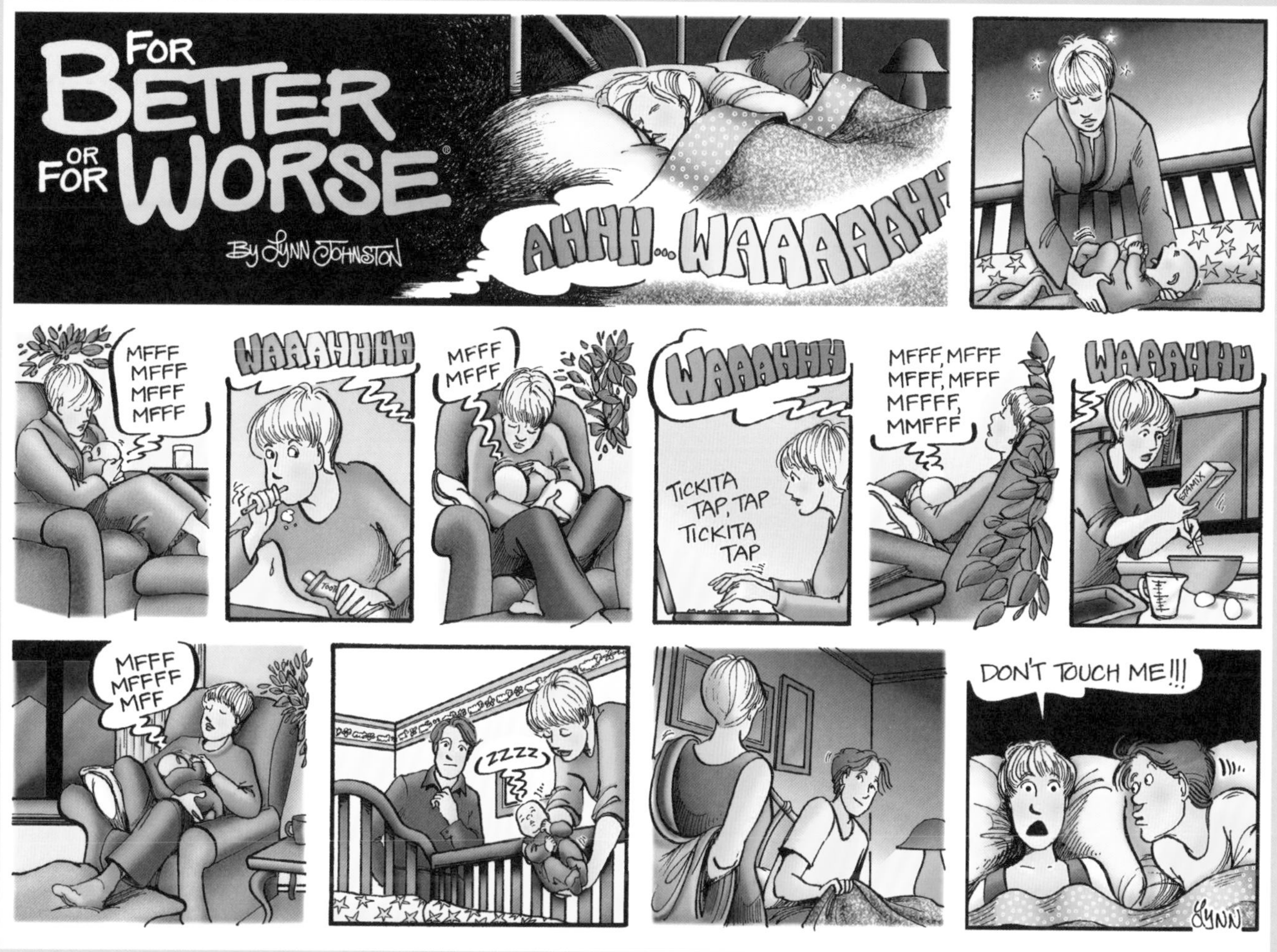
FOR BETTER OR FOR WORSE
BY LYNN JOHNSTON
AHHH... WAAAAAAH
MFFF MFFF MFFF MFFF
WAAAHHHH
MFFF MFFF
WAAAHHH
TICKITA TAP, TAP TICKITA TAP
MFFF, MFFF MFFF, MFFF MFFFF, MMFFF
WAAAHHH
MFFF MFFFF MFF
ZZZZ
DON'T TOUCH ME!!!
LYNN

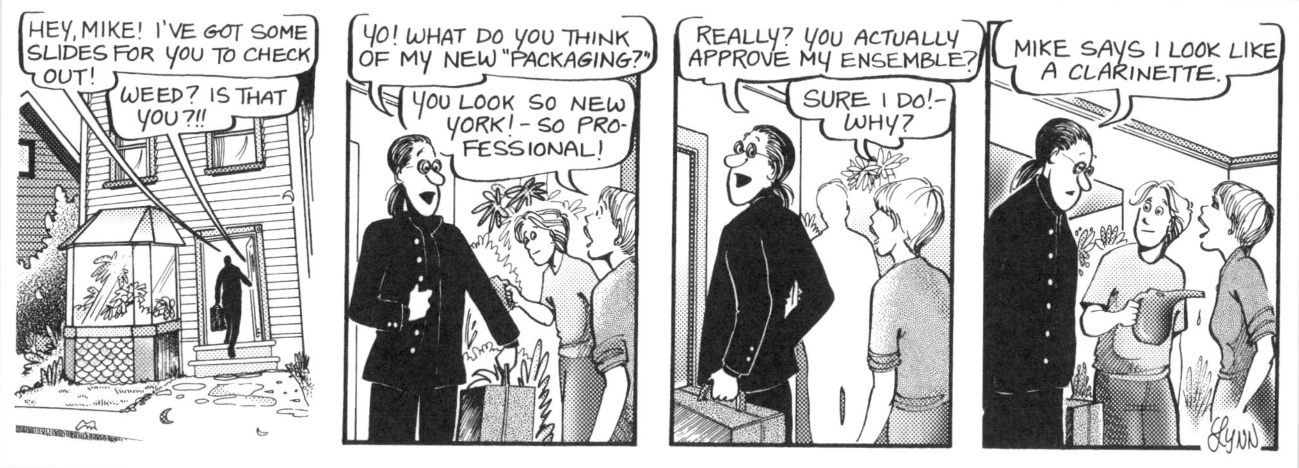
HEY, MIKE! I'VE GOT SOME SLIDES FOR YOU TO CHECK OUT!
WEED? IS THAT YOU?!!
YO! WHAT DO YOU THINK OF MY NEW "PACKAGING?"
YOU LOOK SO NEW YORK! - SO PROFESSIONAL!
REALLY? YOU ACTUALLY APPROVE MY ENSEMBLE?
SURE I DO! - WHY?
MIKE SAYS I LOOK LIKE A CLARINETTE.
LYNN

I CALLED GEORGE STIBBS, DEANNA. HE'LL HAVE HIS HOUSE READY TO SHOW YOU IN A WEEK.

A WEEK?

FIRST HE HAS TO GET ALL HIS PAPER WORK IN ORDER, TALK TO HIS LAWYER AND SO ON.

HE'S BEEN LIVING ALONE FOR SOME TIME. I SUSPECT THERE'S SOME TIDYING UP TO DO. ‡TSK‡ THAT WOULD BE A PRETTY NICE PLACE TO HAVE, ALRIGHT!

YES! I THINK WE COULD DO QUITE WELL IF WE JUST SEVERED THE PROPERTY!

SEVER THE PROPERTY!?

WHERE WOULD I PUT MY TRAINS?!!

FOR BETTER OR FOR WORSE
BY LYNN JOHNSTON

YES, THAT'S YOUR FRIEND ERNIE. HE FLEW A LANCASTER, DIDN'T HE.

YOU SEE? YOU HAVEN'T FORGOTTEN VERY MUCH, JIM!

THANK GOODNESS FOR PHOTOGRAPHS!

YES!

1940-1947

THE COTTAGE AT KAKAWA LAKE!

YES. YES.

OUR TRIP TO ENGLAND

1960-1967

HERE'S YOUR SON'S GRADUATION AND LOOK! ...THE BIRTH OF YOUR FIRST GRANDCHILD!

SO, HOW'S THE HISTORY LESSON GOING, IRIS?

FINE, DEAR, JUST FINE.

WE'VE WORKED OUR WAY UP TO THE MIDDLE AGES!

Growing Up with the Pattersons
An Evolution of Style in For Better or For Worse

Curatorial essay by AMBER LANDGRAFF

Many people know and love the comic strip *For Better or For Worse*. Spanning a 30-year period in the original syndication, with strips written 365 days a year, there are upwards of 10,000 comics in existence. Over the course of the strip's publication, many stylistic changes occurred, taking the comic from a glimpse into the everyday home life of the Patterson family to a rich, expansive comic with three-dimensional characters that seemed more real than fictional. Lynn Johnston has always depicted the Pattersons and their friends with humour, lightness, and a generosity that allowed for an authentic treatment of difficult subject matter. In the comic, moments that could be uncomfortable and not easily discussed were presented with compassion and kindness and handled with Johnston's deft touch. Her use of humour and her willingness to include issues such as divorce, adultery, death, and homosexuality are often held up as examples of how *For Better or For Worse* was a comic ahead of its time.

Johnston's readiness to include stories that reflect the things people face in their lives enhanced the realism of the strip. The comic's successful depiction of realistic situations allowed many readers to feel as though they were looking through a window at their own lives. Events in the strip resonated with readers all across North America. Seeing Elly and her family cope with familiar scenarios contributed to the phenomenal success of the strip.

In Lynn Johnston's archives there are letters upon letters from readers describing how they relate to the comic strip and how their own lives are reflected in the Pattersons' lives. With subjects

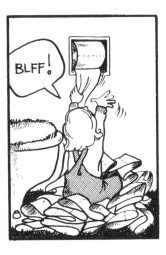

such as pregnancy, family dynamics, sibling rivalry, divorce, puberty, college away from home, first jobs, grandparenthood, retirement, aging, and death, readers came to regard the Pattersons as close friends, even family.

Johnston's decision to have the characters age and develop was significant. Readers who had started following the strip because they identified with Elly, and her struggles as a young mother, could eventually watch the Patterson children age in real time, which allowed for that

One of many examples of multi-cultural secondary characters.

self-identification to continue long into the comic's run. Each daily strip was a way of checking in with characters that had become real for readers. When the comic came to an end in 2008, there was an outpouring of grief from fans, many of whom felt like they were losing close friends.

While the Patterson family may be a classic representation of a white middle-class family, Johnston is also adept at capturing a diverse community with her secondary characters and the background of her comics. Johnston received numerous letters from readers thanking her for including people "like them" in the comics because they rarely saw themselves represented there.

Johnston's faithful representations of people for her characters can be partially attributed to the ways in which Elly, John, Michael, and Elizabeth were, very early on, modelled after her own family. The Pattersons developed over time and became less like Johnston's own family and more characters in their own right; however, the familiarity and realism carried over into the comics. The strength of *For Better or For Worse* was the convincing way in which characters, even the secondary ones, seemed fully formed. Even when characters weren't front and centre in the storyline they were not static figures waiting to be brought back unchanged from their last appearance. Instead, Johnston was able to build rich backstories for her characters, which contributed to the true-to-life quality of the comic. Most characters quickly grew into lives of their own. An example is Elly's friend Connie, who was initially presented as a friendly enemy for Elly but who ultimately became a sympathetic friend struggling with feelings of loneliness as a single mother. In the case

171

of Connie, Johnston did not originally intend the sympathetic turn for her character; it evolved as a product of the realism of her characterizations.

While the initial comics were based on Johnston's family life, writing the strip allowed her to rewrite some moments of her own life in a more hopeful way. For instance, Johnston remarks in her 2004 collection, *Suddenly Silver: Celebrating 25 Years*, when her mother passed away, her brother was unable to be with them; yet, in the comic Uncle Phil was by his mother's side when she passed away. Perhaps one of the most significant of these departures from Johnston's personal narrative was the birth of April. While Johnston herself never had a third child, she was able to realistically portray the experience through Elly. Many readers responded to the accurate depiction of pregnancy in the strip and felt they were able to go through their own pregnancies *with* Elly, whether living the actual experience or reliving memories.

Reading *For Better or For Worse* from the beginning, it is apparent Johnston refines her skill in drawing the comic over time: the comic undergoes substantial changes in how the characters are drawn. Johnston acknowledges in *Suddenly Silver*, an anniversary edition of her comic, she learned about drawing as she went, taking the opportunity for the daily comic when it was offered and then spending time honing her craft. Of course, the speed with which daily comics need to be

produced allowed for occasional mistakes. Sometimes these were drawing errors. Lynn mistakenly drew Elizabeth's hand backwards in the third panel (above). This error slipped past Lynn and her editors and was published in the newspapers on October, 24, 2005. The mistake was caught by a reader and corrected (left) before it was published in Lynn's collection book, *Teaching…Is a Learning Experience.*

There have been occasional disparities between Johnston's intention and the readers' interpretation. In the comic below, her intention was for readers to see John gently nudging Farley with his foot to move him out of the way. Readers interpreted the image as John kicking Farley. A consequence of the comic's large and vocal fan base was that readers were quick to alert Johnston to their upset.

Early comics present a clean and simple drawing style and a slice-of-life view into the Patterson household. However, the characters, while recognizable, are not drawn with the same uniformity that emerged in later strips. There was a clear change in the drawing style as Johnston became more adept with her medium. In the early eighties Johnston was approached about turning her characters into an animated television special. With the production of the animated special, more consistency had to be added to the backgrounds and characters to make it easier for other

An example of Lynn's early work and drawing style.

animators to accurately capture Johnston's style. At this point more attention had to be paid to details such as the height of the characters, facial expressions, and movements. For example, Farley the dog began to move like a real dog, highlighting Johnston's considerable skill at capturing his movements within a static frame. For dog lovers, Farley, one of the most loved characters in the comic, offers an endearing representation of their own dogs without the mess, smell, and food bills. In the comic below, Farley is outside the house trying to get inside. His anxiety as he waits at the door is apparent and, for those fans with dogs, incredibly familiar.

One of many examples of the Patterson's living room and their iconic striped couch.

Once the comic begins to include more details in the treatment of characters, backgrounds, and the like, from there on the character's likenesses are stylized in a more consistent way.

Until this point in the comic there was a freedom and openness in both Johnston's drawing style and with elements such as the background of the house, where, if necessary, rooms could be created and hallways stretched to suit the need of an individual comic. As an example of the transition to continuity of details, the Patterson house was originally based on two separate houses that Johnston lived in. When developing the room plans for the animation, it became necessary to think through how the front of one house would logically flow into the design of the other.

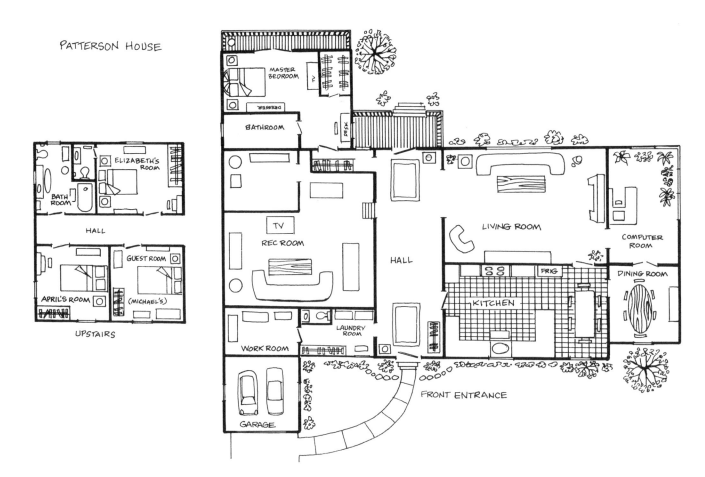

PATTERSON HOUSE

ELIZABETH'S ROOM

BATH ROOM

HALL

APRIL'S ROOM

GUEST ROOM (MICHAEL'S)

UPSTAIRS

MASTER BEDROOM

DRESSER

BATHROOM

DESK

TV

REC ROOM

WORK ROOM

LAUNDRY ROOM

GARAGE

HALL

LIVING ROOM

COMPUTER ROOM

FRIG

KITCHEN

DINING ROOM

FRONT ENTRANCE

Life drastically changed for Johnston when she almost lost her husband, Rod, to a float plane accident in a remote area of Manitoba. The experience affected her so greatly, that in 1986 she depicted John and Uncle Phil in a similar canoe accident (pages 176-177). It was the first time the comic had dealt with a life-and-death situation. This marked a major shift in the comic: longer storylines and realistic events, insecurities, and fears began to enter the comic in a much more significant way. It also presented a shift away from a focus on parenting, household chaos, and family relationships, allowing for more of the real world to seep into the comic. Over several comics, readers watched as Elly anxiously awaited news about John and Uncle Phil's safety. Johnston handled with both depth and humour the uncomfortable insecurity of not knowing where they were and whether they were safe, and for the first time, the fragility of the Pattersons' lives was exposed. Throughout the ordeal, Johnston set *For Better or For Worse* apart from other comics by not guaranteeing the rescue and return of much loved characters. From then on, many other significant storylines covered difficult subject matter, including the child abuse of Michael's friend Gordon, giving birth at home, Farley saving April from drowning and his subsequent death, and perhaps the most often referenced storyline, when Lawrence, one of Michael's closest childhood friends, comes out to Michael and his family (facing page).

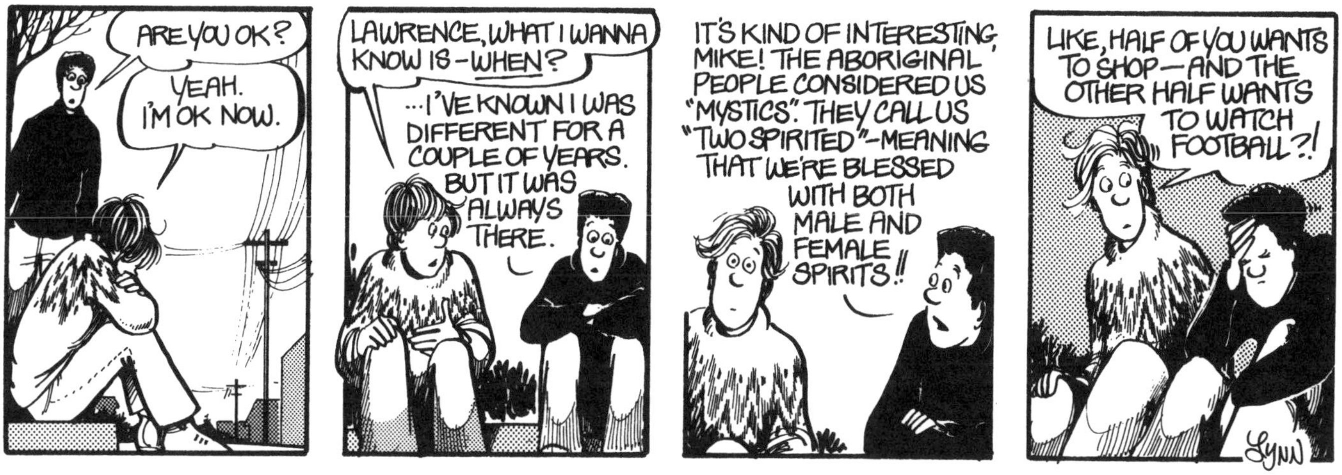
ARE YOU OK?
YEAH. I'M OK NOW.
LAWRENCE, WHAT I WANNA KNOW IS - WHEN?
...I'VE KNOWN I WAS DIFFERENT FOR A COUPLE OF YEARS. BUT IT WAS ALWAYS THERE.
IT'S KIND OF INTERESTING, MIKE! THE ABORIGINAL PEOPLE CONSIDERED US "MYSTICS". THEY CALL US "TWO SPIRITED" - MEANING THAT WE'RE BLESSED WITH BOTH MALE AND FEMALE SPIRITS!!
LIKE, HALF OF YOU WANTS TO SHOP - AND THE OTHER HALF WANTS TO WATCH FOOTBALL?!
LYNN

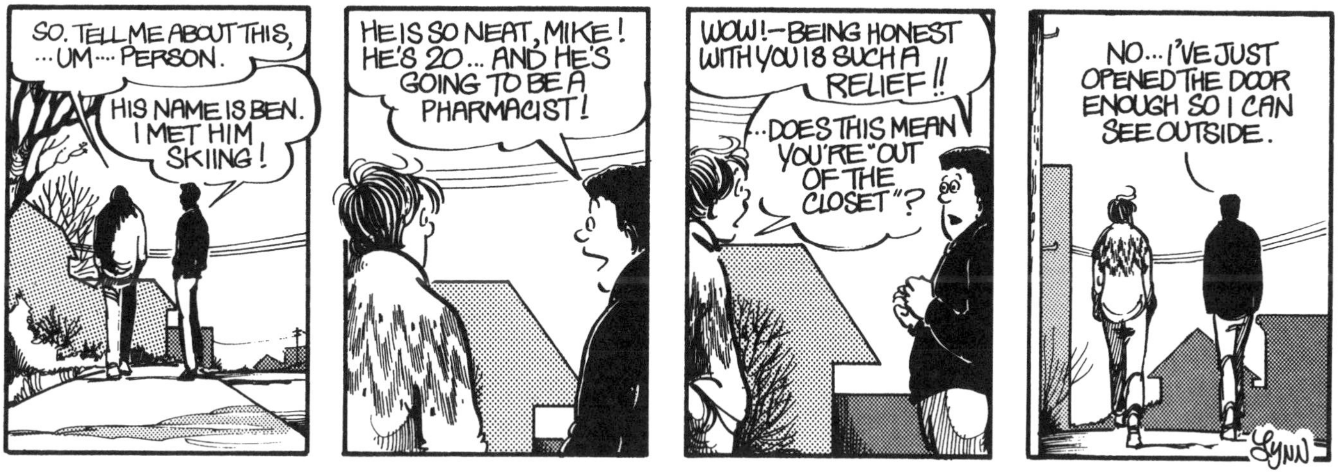
SO. TELL ME ABOUT THIS, ...UM.... PERSON.
HIS NAME IS BEN. I MET HIM SKIING!
HE IS SO NEAT, MIKE! HE'S 20... AND HE'S GOING TO BE A PHARMACIST!
WOW! - BEING HONEST WITH YOU IS SUCH A RELIEF!!
...DOES THIS MEAN YOU'RE "OUT OF THE CLOSET"?
NO... I'VE JUST OPENED THE DOOR ENOUGH SO I CAN SEE OUTSIDE.
LYNN

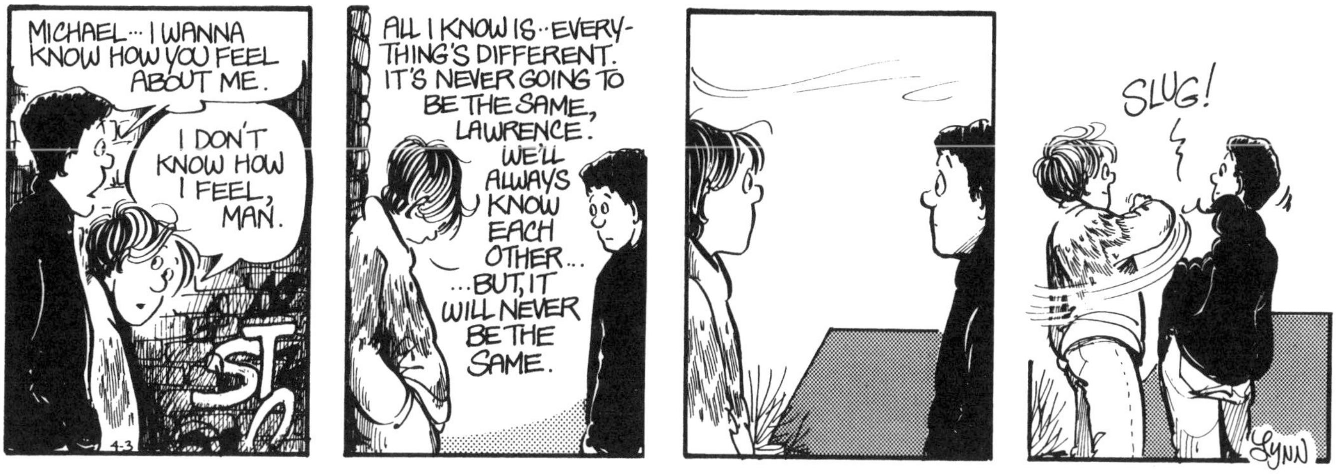
MICHAEL... I WANNA KNOW HOW YOU FEEL ABOUT ME.
I DON'T KNOW HOW I FEEL, MAN.
4-3
ALL I KNOW IS.. EVERYTHING'S DIFFERENT. IT'S NEVER GOING TO BE THE SAME, LAWRENCE. WE'LL ALWAYS KNOW EACH OTHER... ...BUT, IT WILL NEVER BE THE SAME.
SLUG!
LYNN

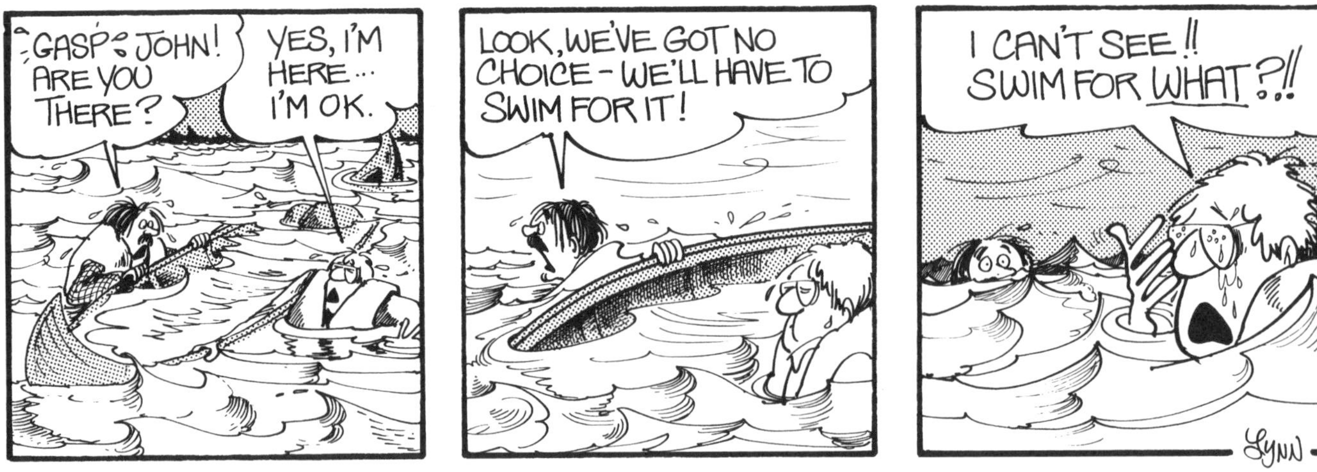

GASP JOHN! ARE YOU THERE?
YES, I'M HERE... I'M OK.
LOOK, WE'VE GOT NO CHOICE - WE'LL HAVE TO SWIM FOR IT!
I CAN'T SEE!! SWIM FOR WHAT?!!
LYNN

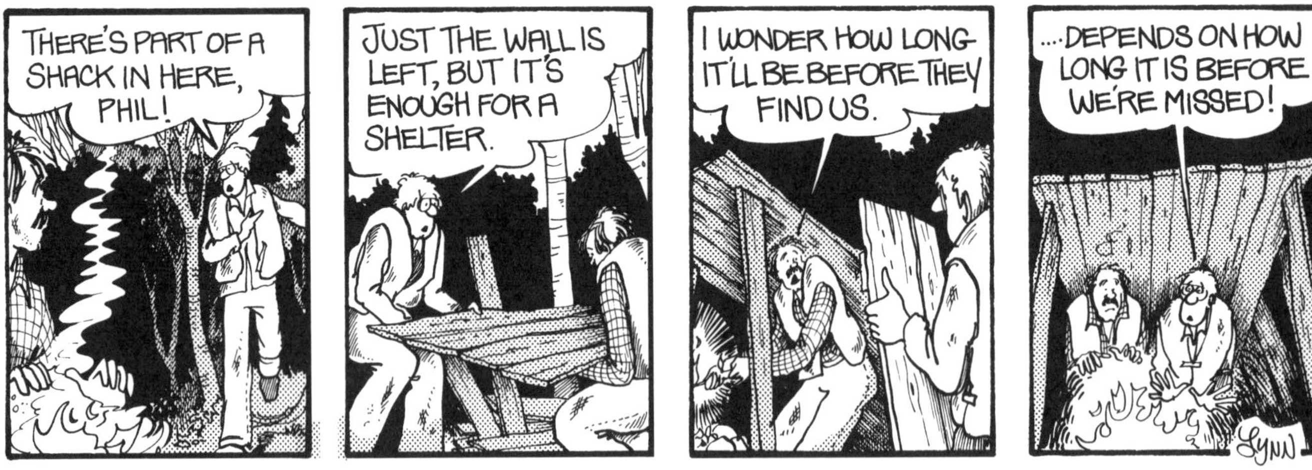

THERE'S PART OF A SHACK IN HERE, PHIL!
JUST THE WALL IS LEFT, BUT IT'S ENOUGH FOR A SHELTER.
I WONDER HOW LONG IT'LL BE BEFORE THEY FIND US.
....DEPENDS ON HOW LONG IT IS BEFORE WE'RE MISSED!
LYNN

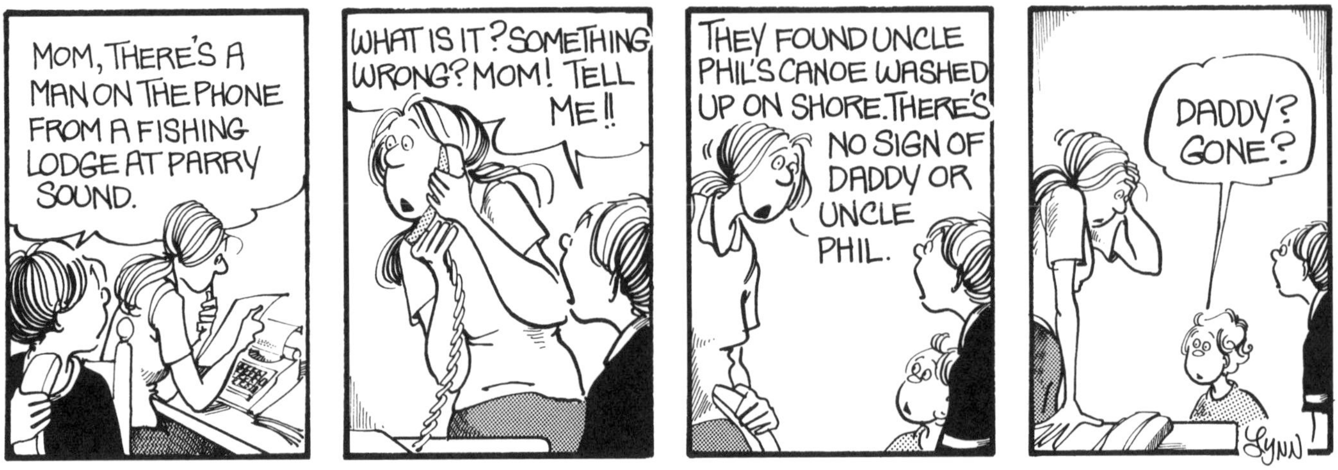

MOM, THERE'S A MAN ON THE PHONE FROM A FISHING LODGE AT PARRY SOUND.
WHAT IS IT? SOMETHING WRONG? MOM! TELL ME!!
THEY FOUND UNCLE PHIL'S CANOE WASHED UP ON SHORE. THERE'S NO SIGN OF DADDY OR UNCLE PHIL.
DADDY? GONE?
LYNN

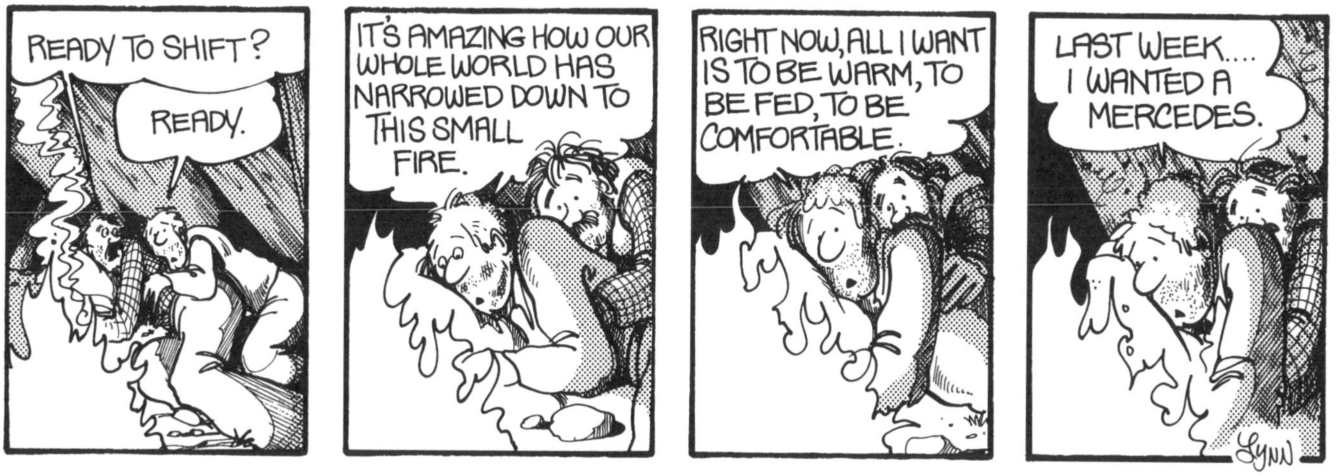
READY TO SHIFT?
READY.
IT'S AMAZING HOW OUR WHOLE WORLD HAS NARROWED DOWN TO THIS SMALL FIRE.
RIGHT NOW, ALL I WANT IS TO BE WARM, TO BE FED, TO BE COMFORTABLE.
LAST WEEK.... I WANTED A MERCEDES.
LYNN

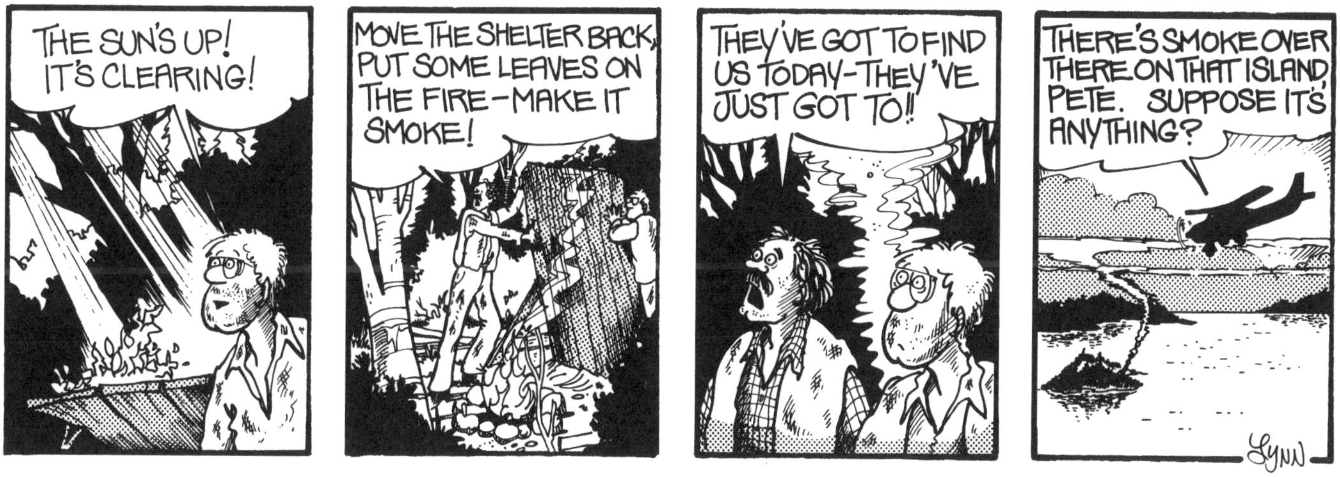
THE SUN'S UP! IT'S CLEARING!
MOVE THE SHELTER BACK, PUT SOME LEAVES ON THE FIRE - MAKE IT SMOKE!
THEY'VE GOT TO FIND US TODAY - THEY'VE JUST GOT TO!!
THERE'S SMOKE OVER THERE ON THAT ISLAND, PETE. SUPPOSE IT'S ANYTHING?
LYNN

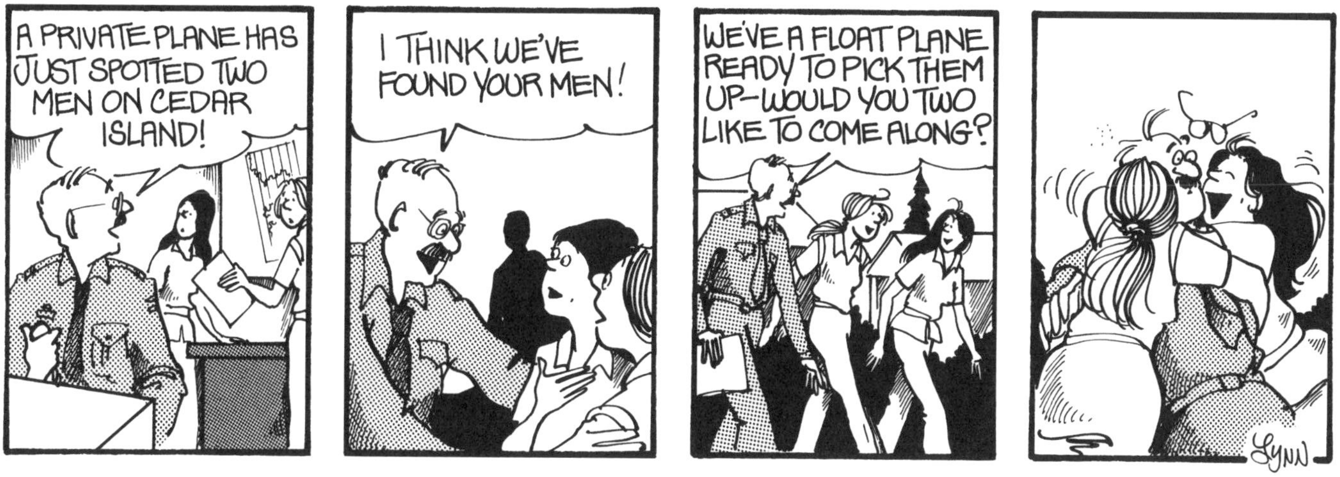
A PRIVATE PLANE HAS JUST SPOTTED TWO MEN ON CEDAR ISLAND!
I THINK WE'VE FOUND YOUR MEN!
WE'VE A FLOAT PLANE READY TO PICK THEM UP - WOULD YOU TWO LIKE TO COME ALONG?
LYNN

As the comic went on and the characters continued to age, Johnston's drawing approach began another shift. Michael and Elizabeth moved away to college and started their adult lives, and the comical style in the earlier comics of their youth took on a more realistic treatment. The comic became even more detailed with more attention than ever before to the background settings, and the characters were drawn with more life-like accuracy. This development can be partially attributed to Johnston's growing team; she was working with people who could support her in her process. Johnston was able to delegate the background designs to Laura Piché and spend more time drawing the characters. However, the increasing realism can also be seen as a logical progression in her style as she continued to develop as an artist.

When it came time to end the comic, Johnston chose to offer a wrap-up for the Patterson family. Ending with the wedding between Elizabeth and her childhood sweetheart Anthony made many fans, who had always hoped they would end up together, very happy. At the same time, fans who had grown up with the comic, and were themselves approaching old age and retirement, had been looking forward to following the Pattersons into their old age; they were dismayed to find

ELLY, IF WE COULD GO BACK IN TIME, I MEAN ... IF I ASKED YOU TO...

YES, JOHN

... WITH ALL MY HEART, I WOULD!

ELLY AND JOHN PATTERSON RETIRED TO TRAVEL, TO READ, TO VOLUNTEER IN THEIR COMMUNITY AND TO HELP RAISE THEIR GRANDCHILDREN!

GRANDPA JIM LIVED TO WELCOME ANTHONY AND ELIZABETH'S FIRST CHILD, JAMES ALLEN. JIM PASSED AWAY AT THE AGE OF 89, WITH HIS WIFE, IRIS, AT HIS SIDE.

ELIZABETH CONTINUES TO WORK AS A TEACHER. SHE'S DEVOTED TO HER WORK AND TO HER FAMILY, LOVING ANTHONY MORE EACH DAY.

ANTHONY MANAGES THE MAYES MOTORS EMPIRE, HAS DRAWN HIS BRIDE INTO BALLROOM DANCING, AND LOOKS FORWARD SOMEDAY TO OPENING A SMALL BED-AND-BREAKFAST.

MICHAEL PATTERSON HAD 4 BOOKS IN PRINT BEFORE SIGNING A FILM CONTRACT. HE CONTINUES TO WORK WITH JOSEF WEEDER AND TO WRITE FROM HOME - WHERE HE SAYS HIS INSPIRATION AND HIS CONFIDENCE LIE.

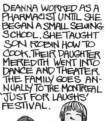

DEANNA WORKED AS A PHARMACIST UNTIL SHE BEGAN A SMALL SEWING SCHOOL. SHE TAUGHT SON ROBIN HOW TO COOK. THEIR DAUGHTER MEREDITH WENT INTO DANCE AND THEATER. THE FAMILY GOES ANNUALLY TO THE MONTREAL 'JUST FOR LAUGHS' FESTIVAL.

APRIL PATTERSON GRADUATED FROM UNIVERSITY WITH A DEGREE IN VETERINARY MEDICINE. HER LOVE OF HORSES LED HER TO A JOB IN CALGARY AND AN OPPORTUNITY TO WORK WITH THE CALGARY STAMPEDE. COUNTRY LIVING AND A COUNTRY BOY KEEP HER "OUT WEST"!

THE EXTENDED FAMILIES, FRIENDS AND ACQUAINTANCES OF THE PATTERSONS CONTINUE TO LIVE AND GROW, LOVE AND LAUGH AND EXPERIENCE LIFE AS WE DO....

AS IF PART OF A COMPLEX NOVEL, WHOSE PAGES ARE CAREFULLY CRAFTED AND THEN TURNED BY ANOTHER HAND.

THANK YOU - TO MY SYNDICATE, PUBLISHER, FAMILY, STAFF, READERS AND FRIENDS FOR ENCOURAGING, GUIDING AND ACCOMPANYING ME THESE PAST 29 YEARS - AS "FOR BETTER OR FOR WORSE" GREW FROM SIMPLE SKETCHES TO AN INTRICATE "SAGA" INVOLVING MANY CHARACTERS. MOST OF THIS HAS BEEN FICTION; SOME HAS COME FROM LIFE. I WAS GIVEN THE OPPORTUNITY TO "DRAW FROM EXPERIENCE" AND, WHAT AN EXPERIENCE IT'S BEEN! IN LOOKING BACK, I CAN ONLY SAY ... IT'S BEEN WONDERFUL!!

Lynn Johnston

the comic ending. In Johnston's archives, the letters she received at the end of the comic carry many of the same responses about the similarities readers saw between the Pattersons and their own families. The letters share many life stories that the strip reflected: the birth of children, watching them grow and then having families of their own, losing parents and the grief that follows. Perhaps most importantly, these letters reveal how much the Pattersons would be missed. The comic ends happily; yet, as always, it also ends realistically. The final strip, published on August 31, 2008, gives a peek into the Patterson family's future and allows a form of closure to lives of the characters that readers knew and loved.

Acknowledgements

Unless otherwise noted, all direct quotations of Lynn Johnston are from personal interviews with the author held between October 27 and December 18, 2014.

Quotations on pages 22, 23, 24, 25, 56, 60, 61, 64, 66, 69, 80, 81, 91, 100, 101, 109, 117, and 135 are taken from Lynn Johnston, *A Look Inside "For Better or For Worse": The 10th Anniversary Collection* (Kansas City, MO: Andrews McMeel, 1989).

The quotation on page 26 is taken from a personal email from Unity Bainbridge to the author on November 15, 2014.

Quotations on pages 27 and 114 are taken from Lynn Johnston, *It's the Thought That Counts: Fifteenth Anniversary Collection* (Kansas City, MO: Andrews and McMeel, 1989).

Quotations on pages 33, 94, and 147 are taken from Lynn Johnston, *The Lives Behind the Lines: 20 Years of "For Better or For Worse"* (Kansas City, MO: Andrews McMeel, 1999).

The quotation on page 52 is taken from Patrick McDonnell, foreword to *Sergio Aragonés: Five Decades of His Finest Works*, by Sergio Aragonés (Philadelphia, PA: Running Press, 2010).

Quotations on pages 57, 59, and 60-61 are taken from Lynn Johnston, *It's One Thing After Another: "For Better or For Worse" 4th Treasury* (Kansas City, MO: Andrews McMeel, 2014).

Quotations on pages 112, 121, 140-141, and 148 are taken from Lynn Johnston, *Suddenly Silver: Celebrating 25 Years of "For Better or For Worse"* (Kansas City, MO: Andrews McMeel, 2004).

The quotation on page 123 is taken from Lynn Johnston, *Making Ends Meet: "For Better or For Worse" 3rd Treasury* (Kansas City, MO: Andrews McMeel, 2013).

The quotation on page 133 is taken from "About the NCS," National Cartoonist Society, accessed December 3, 2014, http://www.reuben.org/about.

The quotation on page 152 is taken from Lynn Johnston, *Something Old, Something New: "For Better or For Worse" 1st Treasury* (Kansas City, MO: Andrews McMeel, 2010).

Bibliography

Unless otherwise stated the following are authored by Lynn Johnston and published by Andrews McMeel, Kansas City.

Full descriptive entries can be found at: http://www.fborfw.com/behind_the_scenes/bibliography

COLLECTIONS

David, We're Pregnant! (1974)

Hi Mom! Hi Dad! (1977)

Do They Ever Grow Up? (1978)

I've Got the One-More-Washload Blues (1981)

Is This "One of Those Days," Daddy? (1982)

"It Must be Nice to Be Little" (1983)

More Than a Month of Sundays (1983)

Just One More Hug (1984)

Our Sunday Best (1984)

The Last Straw (1985)

Keep the Home Fries Burning (1986)

It's All Downhill From Here (1987)

Pushing 40 (1988)

If This Is a Lecture, How Long Will It Be? (1990)

What, Me Pregnant? (1991)

Things Are Looking Up… (1992)

"There Goes My Baby!" (1993)

Starting From Scratch (1995)

Love Just Screws Everything Up (1996)

Growing Like a Weed (1997)

Middle Age Spread (1998)

Sunshine & Shadow (1999)

The Big 5-0 (2000)

All About April: Our Little Girl Grew Up! (2001)

Graduation: A Time for Change (2001)

Family Business (2002)

With this Ring (2003)

Reality Check (2003)

Striking a Chord (2005)

Never Wink at a Worried Woman (2005)

She's Turning Into One of Them (2006)

Teaching…Is a Learning Experience! (2007)

Seniors' Discount (2007)

Home Sweat Home (2008)

Just A Simple Wedding (2009)

RETROSPECTIVES

A Look Inside…For Better or For Worse: The 10th Anniversary Collection (1989)

It's the Thought That Counts…Fifteenth Anniversary Collection (1994)

Remembering Farley: A Tribute to the Life of Our Favourite Cartoon Dog (1996)

The Lives Behind the Lines…20 Years of For Better or For Worse (1999)

Suddenly Silver: Celebrating 25 Years of For Better or For Worse (2004)

Something Old, Something New: For Better or For Worse 1st Treasury (2011)

In the Beginning, There Was Chaos: For Better or For Worse 2nd Treasury (2012)

Making Ends Meet: For Better or For Worse 3rd Treasury (2013)

It's One Thing After Another! For Better or For Worse 4th Treasury (2014)

STORYBOOKS

Lynn Johnston and Beth Cruikshank, *Farley Follows His Nose* (New York: The Bowen Press, a division of HarperCollins, 2009)

Lynn Johnston and Beth Cruikshank, *Farley and the Lost Bone* (2011)

WITH ANDIE PARTON

Wags and Kisses: A For Better or For Worse Little Book (2001)

Graduation…Just the Beginning! A For Better or For Worse Little Book (2003)

Leaving Home (2003)

So You're Going to Be a Grandma! A Better or For Worse Book (2005)

I Love My Grandpa! A For Better or For Worse Book (2006)

OTHER

Isn't He Beautiful? A For Better or For Worse Little Book (2000)

Isn't She Beautiful? A For Better or For Worse Little Book (2000)

A Perfect Christmas: A For Better or For Worse Little Book (2001)

Lynn Johnston and Brenda Wegmann, *Laugh 'n' Learn Spanish* (New York: McGraw-Hill, 2004)

Illustration Credits

Unless otherwise indicated, images appear courtesy of Lynn Johnston.

The painting *Little Indian Patient* by Unity Bainbridge (page 25) is used by permission of Unity Bainbridge. The illustration of the office party scene by Virgil Partch (page 42) is from the book *VIP Tosses a Party* and used by permission of Anna Partch Couch. "News Item: Probe Begins as P.G.E. Train Refuses to Stop for Passengers" by Len Norris (page 43) is used by permission of Stephen Norris. "Dancer" by Jules Feiffer (page 48) is used by permission of © Jules Feiffer. The illustrations on pages 51 and 52 from *MAD* magazine are by Al Jaffee (™ & © E.C. Publications, Inc.) and Sergio Aragonés (From MAD # 263 © E.C. Publications Inc.), respectively, and are used by permission of E.C. Publications Inc. The photo on page 59 of Cecily Sell and Lynn Johnston is used by permission of Cecily Sell Mitchell. The photo on page 75 of Bernhard Thor is used by permission of sculptor, wood carver, stone mason, and fine artist Bernhard Thor. The photo on page 82 of Andie Parton and Lynn Johnston is used by permission of Andie Parton. The photo on page 135 of Lynn Johnston with Charles Schulz and Cathy Guisewite is used by permission of Cathy Guisewite and Jean Schulz.

Index

A

Abbott and Costello (cartoon) 57-58
Andrews, Jim 100, 106
Andrews McMeel Publishing 144
Aragonés, Sergio 52-53
Art Gallery of Sudbury 14

B

Bacharach, Burt 109
Baez, Joan 49
Bainbridge, Unity (aunt) 25-26, 75
Baskin, Bernard 89, 94
Baskin, Marjorie 68-69, 76, 79, 83, 89, 94, 106
Beard, Alpine 59
Beard, Cecil 59
Bestest Present, The (TV special) 60
Best of Norris, The (book) 43
Beth (sister-in-law) 94-95
Blondie (comic strip) 136
Blushbottom Memoirs, The (book) 35
Brenne, Kathryn 159, 162
Brown, Charlie (character) 45
Bugs Bunny (character) 40
Burlington ON 69, 70

C

Caine, Anthony (character) 152, 180
Canada's Walk of Fame 156-157
Canadian Broadcasting Corporation 59-60
Canadian Children's Annual, The 96
Canawest Films 57-59
cartoons 40
Cat in the Hat, The (book) 31
Cathy (comic strip) 100
Chaplin, Charlie 40, 52
CHCH TV 60, 91
Chedoke Hospital 64, 66
"Claude and the Woodpile" (poem) 118-120

Cockshott, Dr. 64
Collingwood ON 21, 22, 124
comic books 40, 41, 46

D

Daffy Duck (character) 40
David, Hal 109
David, We're Pregnant! (book) 89-90, 96-97
Davis, Jim 134, 136
Dennis the Menace (comic strip) 130
Dick Tracy (comic strip) 41, 46
Different Drummer Books 70
Disney, Walt 41
Disney Studios 59
Do They Ever Grow Up? (book) 97, 99
Don (brother-in-law) 94
Drucker, Mort 51
Dundas ON 69, 70, 72, 76, 92, 137
Dundas Valley Journal 72

E

Eggbert (book) 89
England 21
Enjo, Carol (character) 126
Enkin, Eleanor 89
Enkin, Dr. Murray 76-79, 89, 102

F

Farley (character) 70, 141, 173, 174, 176
Farley (pet) 69-70, 76, 83
Feiffer, Jules 47-49
First Nations 25, 92
"Fish Pattern" (dress pattern) 162
For Better or For Worse
   business 130-131
   cartoon 137
   end of 13, 146-149, 151, 152, 171
   ethnicity 141, 170-171

evolution of strip 173-175, 180

expansion 116

Farley's death 141, 144, 176

in newspapers 15

inspirations 121, 126, 127, 138

Lawrence's coming out 140-141, 144, 176

online 15

origins 100-102, 106-109, 112

promotion 117

publisher 144

reader feedback 141-143, 169, 171, 180, 181

readership 15

real-life issues 140, 141, 169, 170, 176

rerunning the strip 152

success 136

Forest (painting) 155

Franks, Doug (first husband) 58-60, 69, 70, 72, 73, 76, 79, 80

Franks, Lynn (pen name) 89

Freberg, Stan 34

Funny Birds (paintings) 160-161

Funny Dog (painting) 158

G

Garden Village ON 129

Garfield (comic strip) 134, 136

George of the Jungle (cartoon) 60

Goon Show, The 34

Graham, Bob 124

Guisewite, Cathy 100, 102, 106, 134, 135

Gyro Gearloose (cartoon) 59

H

Hadway, Kate (Johnston) (daughter) 100, 102, 107, 115, 126, 140, 151, 156, 157, 159

Hadway, Laura (granddaughter) 155

Hamilton ON 60, 61, 80

Hamilton Airport 92

Hamilton General Hospital 61-64

Hamilton Spectator 61

Hanna-Barbera 57-60

Hefner, Hugh 46

Herman (comic strip) 136

Hi Mom! Hi Dad! (book) 96, 97, 98

Hindmarch, Mrs. 28

J

Jacobs, Frank 52

Jaffee, Al 51, 53

Jansen, Elly 107-108

Jansen, Lois 108

Janveaux, Malia 162

Jay Ward Studios 59

Johnston, Aaron (son) 76, 78-81, 83, 92-94, 107, 115, 126, 140, 151

Johnston, Lynn

  archives 156, 169, 180

  books 89-90, 97

  business 130-133, 149, 151, 156, 157, 159

    fashion 156-157, 159, 162-163

    patterns (textile) 159, 162-163

  Canada's Walk of Fame 156-157

  Canawest Films 57-59

  childhood 21-35, 40-54

  end of strip 146-149, 151-152

  evolution of strip 180

  first marriage 58-60, 69, 70, 72-74, 76, 79, 80

  For Better or For Worse 100-102, 106-109, 112, 126, 136, 170

  freelance work 72, 76, 78-80, 83, 90, 92

  Hamilton General Hospital 61-64

  humour 27

  influences 13, 23-26, 31-34, 40-54

  McMaster University 64-69, 72, 76, 90

  other cartoonists 133-136

  painting 146, 155

  publicity 116, 117, 140

  realism in strip 171, 172, 176, 180

  retirement 155-156

  Reuben Award 134

  school 27-35, 46, 54

  second marriage 92-94, 100, 124, 126, 151

  snarkers 147-148

  spasmodic torticollis 150-151

  Standard Engravers 80-81, 90

  success 21

  Vancouver School of Art 55-58

  website 147

Johnston, Rod (second husband) 91-94, 96, 100, 107, 114, 123, 124, 126, 132, 133, 149-151, 176

Johnston, Ruth (mother-in-law) 93, 115, 116, 123, 126

Johnston, Tom (father-in-law) 93, 115, 116, 123, 126, 156

Johnstons, The (first title for *For Better or For Worse*) 106

Jones, Spike 34

K

Kansas City MO 100, 130, 133

Keaton, Buster 52

Ketcham, Hank 130

Keystone Kops 40

Klotz, Mr. 121

L

Lansky, Bruce 97, 106

Le Pew, Pepé (character) 40

Lehrer, Tom 34

Li'l Abner (comic strip) 41, 46

Little Dancer (comic strip) 47-48

Little Indian Patient (Unity Bainbridge) 25

Little Lulu (comic book) 50

Los Angeles CA 58, 59

Lowney, Mr. 107, 108

Luggsworth, Brad (character) 139

Lynn Lake MB 100, 102, 106, 114-117, 121, 123, 127, 137

M

MAD magazine 49, 50-53

Martin, Don 51

Mary Tyler Moore Show, The 143

Matchette, Karen 130-132

Mayes, Gordon (character) 176

McCaulay, Ted (character) 122

McLaren, Norman 57

McMaster University 64, 67, 68, 76, 90

McMaster University Medical Centre 64-67, 69, 72

McMeel, John 100

Meadowbrook Press 97

Mickey Mouse (character) 41, 50

Miss Peach (comic strip) 46

Montreal QC 25, 33

Mowat, Farley 69, 70

N

National Cartoonists Society 133-134

National Film Board 57

New Yorker, The 46-47

Nichols, Anne (character) 80, 121, 126

Nipissing First Nation 129

Nipissing University 127-129

Norris, Len 43-44, 53

North Bay ON 124, 126, 127, 129, 130, 140, 141

North Vancouver BC 22, 33, 40, 50, 58, 75, 107

North Vancouver Senior Secondary High School 33, 34, 55

O

O'Brien, Dorothy 144

Odeon Theatre 40

Ottawa ON 124

Our Gang 40

P

Partch, Virgil (VIP) 41-42, 50, 53

Parton, Adrienne (Andie) 82-83

Parton, Christopher 82

Parton, Stephen 82

patterns (textile) 159, 162-163

Patterson, April (character) 70, 138, 172, 176

Patterson, Carrie (character) 93

Patterson, Deanna (Sobinski) (character) 143

Patterson, Elizabeth (character) 107, 127, 128, 142, 152, 171, 173, 180

Patterson, Elly (character) 15, 80, 94, 107-110, 117, 121, 122, 123, 126, 132, 146, 169-172

Patterson, John (character) 92, 94, 107, 122, 146, 151, 171, 173, 176

Patterson, Michael (character) 107, 140, 142, 143, 171, 176, 180

Patterson, William (character) 93

Peanuts (comic strip) 41, 45, 46, 134

Piché, Laura 180

Playboy 32, 46-47

Poirier, Connie (character) 81, 91, 123, 126, 171, 172

Poirier, Lawrence (character) 140, 176

Potter, Dr. Paul 63, 64

R

Reader's Digest 46
Reuben Awards 133-134
Rex Morgan M.D. (comic strip) 46
Reznick, Monica (Bainbridge) (aunt) 25
Richards, Jim (character) 23, 142-143
Richards, Marian (character) 23
Richards, Phil (character) 24, 172, 176
Ridgway, Alan (brother) 22, 24, 30, 94, 172
Ridgway, Mervyn (father) 21, 22, 27, 40-43, 46, 74-76
Ridgway, Ursula (Bainbridge) (mother) 21-23, 25, 26, 29, 42, 50, 74, 76, 94, 107, 108, 124, 172
Rocky and Bullwinkle (cartoon) 60
Roush, Sue 144, 155
Rupert (book) 31

S

Sackett, David 66-67
Salem, Lee 100, 102, 106, 112, 117, 140, 144, 155
Schultz, Charles 45, 134-135, 146
Schultz, Jeannie 134-135
Scrooge McDuck (comic) 59
Seattle WA 59
Secombe, Harry 34
Sell, Cecily (Beard) 58, 59
Seton Portage BC 75
Shazzan (cartoon) 57
Silverstein, Shel 32
Sneyd, Doug 46
Spy vs. Spy 51
Standard Engravers 80-81, 90
Stibbs, George 29-32
Stolberg, Dr. Harald 62-64
Strang, Kevin 159
Suddenly Silver (book) 145, 172
Sue the librarian (character) 126
Super Chicken (cartoon) 60
Sutherland Junior High School 33

T

Tate, Miss 27
Teaching…Is a Learning Experience (book) 173
Theriault, Thérèse 32-34
Thor, Bernhard 75
Toronto ON 21, 60, 74, 92, 96, 124, 130, 156

U

Unger, Jim 136
Universal Press Syndicate 100, 101, 106, 112, 114, 117, 130, 140, 144, 152, 156

V

van Doleweerd, Stephanie 156
Vancouver BC 58, 60, 69, 74, 76, 151
Vancouver School of Art 25, 55-58
Vancouver Sun 43
VandeBoncoeur, Michael 34-35, 140
Victoria BC 93
VIP Tosses a Party (book) 42

W

Walker, Ken 57
Walsingham ON 69
Ward, Jay 60
Watson, Mrs. 34-35
Weir, Dennis 90, 91
West Vancouver BC 24
When I Was Lindy (book) 27, 30
Where the Sidewalk Ends (book) 32
Willis, Paul 34, 35, 140
Willy (pet) 141
Wilson, Tom 136
Winnie-the-Pooh (book) 31
"Wives and Lovers" (song) 109
Wotton, Greg 156

Y

Young, Charlotte 136
Young, Dean 136

Z

Ziggy (comic strip) 136